Table of Contents

Back To The Bible: Bible Basic

Commentary by Thru The Bible with J. Vernon McGee

By Charles Lloyd Jr.

REJOICE
Essential Publishing

Charles Lloyd Jr/Rejoice Essential Publishing

PO BOX 512

Effingham, SC 29541

www.republishing.org

Unless otherwise indicated, scripture is taken from the King James Version.

Back To The Bible/Charles Lloyd Jr

McGee, J., 1998. Thru the Bible with J. Vernon McGee. Nashville: T. Nelson.

ISBN-13: 978-1-956775-47-1

Introduction

The Book of Revelation

Introduction

Outline

Writer: *John The Apostle*
Dated about AD 95

Theories of Interpretation: This book has many approaches, but these can be divided into four major systems.

1. **Preterist theory:** All of the revelation has been fulfilled in the past. It had to do with local references in John's day and with the days of either Nero or Domitian. The purpose of the Book of Revelation was to bring comfort to the persecuted church and was written in symbols that the Christians of that period would understand.

2. **Historical theory:** Fulfillment of Revelation is going on in the church's history from John's day to the present time. It is obvious that the Book of Revelation is prophetic.

3. **History-Spiritual Theory:** It's a refinement of historical theory. This theory states that the two beasts are imperial and provincial Rome and that the point of the book is to encourage Christians. According to this theory, Revelation has been largely fulfilled and contains only spiritual lessons for the church today.

4. **Futurist theory:** This theory holds that the Book of Revelation is primarily prophetic and yet futurist, especially from Revelation 4 onto the end of the book. This is the view of all premillennialists and is the view that we accept and present.

Now there are six striking and singular features of the Book of Revelation.

1. It's the only prophetic book in the New Testament. There are seventeen prophetic books in the Old Testament and only this one in the New Testament.

2. John, the writer, reaches further back into eternity's past than any other writer in Scripture *(John 1:1)*. He reaches farther on into eternity's future in the Book of Revelation.

3. Special blessing is promised to the readers of this book *(Revelation 1:3)*. Likewise, a warning is issued to those who tamper with its contents *(Revelation 22:18-19)*.

4. Revelation is not a sealed book *(Revelation 22:10)* in contrast to *Daniel 12:9*. It is a revelation (apocalypse), which is an unveiling.

5. It is a series of visions expressed in symbols that deal with reality. The literal interpretation is always preferred unless John makes it clear that it is otherwise.

6. This book is like a great union Station where the great trunk lines of prophecy come in from other portion of scripture. Revelation does not originate but consummates. It is imperative to get a right understanding of the book to be able to trace each great subject of prophecy from the first reference to this terminal.

Now there are ten great subjects of prophecy that find their consummation here.

1. The Lord Jesus Christ is the subject of the book. The subject is not the beasts nor the bowls of wrath, but the sin-bearer. The first mention of Him was in *Genesis 3:15* as the seed of the woman.

2. The church does not live in the Old Testament. It's first mentioned by the Lord Jesus in *Matthew 16:18.*

3. The resurrection and the translation of the saint (*see John 14:1-14; 1 Thess. 4:13-18; 1 Cor. 15:51-52).*

4. The Great Tribulation is spoken of back in *Deuteronomy 4,* where God says that His people would be in tribulation.

5. Satan and evil (see *Ezek. 28:11-18).*

6. The "*man of sin*" (see *Ezek. 28:1-10)*

7. The course and the end of apostate Christendom (see *Dan. 2:31-45).*

8. The beginning course and the *"times of the Gentiles"* (see *Dan. 2:37-45; Luke 21:24)*. The Lord Jesus said that Jerusalem would be of the Gentiles are fulfilled.

9. The second coming of Christ. According to *Jude 14-15*, Enoch spoke of that which takes us back to the time of the Genesis record.

10. Israel's covenant begins with the covenant God made with Abraham in *Genesis 12:1-3*. God promised Israel fine things, and God says in Revelation that He will fulfill them all.

The Book of Revelation is not a difficult book. Actually, it is the most orderly book in the Bible and there is no reason to misunderstand it. This is what I mean: It divides itself. John puts down the instructions given to him by Christ, *Rev. 1:19* –past, present, and future. Then the book further divides itself into a series of seven, each division as orderly as possible.

To those who claim that it is all symbolic and beyond our understanding, the book of Revelation is to be taken literally. Also, it will be symbolic of reality and the reality will be more real than the symbol for the simple reason that John uses symbols to describe reality. In our study of the book, that is an all-important principle to follow. Lets allow Revelation say what it wants to say.

Now the church is set before us in the figure of seven churches which were real churches in existence in John's day. John was speaking about local situations and the history of the church as a whole. Then after chapter 3, the church is not mentioned anymore. The church is not the subject again in the entire Book of Revelation.

Well, it leaves the earth, goes to heaven and there it appears as the Bride of Christ. When we see her in the last part of Revelation, she is not the church but the Bride. Then the beginning of Chapter 4, everything is definitely in the future from our vantage point at the present time. So when anyone reaches in and pulls out a revelation, some vision about famine or wars or anything or that sort, it just does not fit into the picture of our day. We need to let John tell it like it is. In fact, we need to let the whole Bible speak to us like that- just let it say what it wants to say.

Therefore, we must be very sure that all new truth comes from a correct interpretation of the Word of God.

The subject of this book is very important to see. To emphasize and reemphasize it, let us direct our attention to chapter 1, verse 1— *"The Revelation of Jesus Christ, which God gave unto him, to shew unto his servants the things which must shortly come to pass."* This book is a revelation of Jesus Christ. In the Gospel, we see Him in the days of His flesh, but they do not give the full revelation of Jesus Christ.

In the Gospels, we see Him in humiliation. In the Book of Revelation, we see Him in glory. We see Him in charge of everything that takes place. He is in full command. This is the unveiling of Jesus Christ. Interestingly, Genesis opens the Bible not only with a global view but with a universal view.

"In the beginning, God created the heaven and the earth (Gen. 1:1)." The Bible closes with another global and universal book. The Revelation shows what God is going to do with His universe and with His creatures. There is no other book quite like this.

Outline

I. The Person of Jesus Christ– Christ in Glory–Ch. 1

II. The Possession of Jesus Christ – The Church in the world. –Ch. 2-3

III. The Program of Jesus Christ–The scene in Heaven. –Ch. 4-22.

Chapter 1

Theme: *The person of Jesus Christ.*

The Title of the Book

The Revelation of Jesus Christ, which God gave unto him, to shew unto his servants things which must shortly come to pass; and he sent and signified it by his angel unto his servant John *(Rev.1:1)*.

First, please note that the title of this book is Revelation – singular, not plural.

"To shew unto his servants things which must shortly come to pass." Seal not the saying of the prophecy of this book: for the time is at hand *(Rev. 22:10)*. It is not a sealed book: it is open and to be understood in our day. This is in contrast to the prophecy in the Book of Daniel, which Daniel was instructed to seal. Our Lord Jesus gave what are known as the *"mystery parables."*

In the Gospels, we have only the half story. We need the Book of Revelation because it is the consummation of it. It can be understood only if the Spirit of God is our teacher, but the Book of Revelation takes off the veil so we can see Christ in His unveiled beauty, power, and glory. This book is the opposite of a secret or a mystery, It is a disclosure of a secret and it is called prophecy in the next verse.

The Revelation of Jesus Christ, which God gave unto him, to shew unto his servants things which must shortly come to pass; and he sent and signified it by his angel unto his servant John [Rev.1:1].

"To show" means by word picture, symbols, and direct and indirect representations.

"And he sent and signified it." That is, he used symbols. Keep in mind that the symbols are symbolic of reality. Peter gave a great rule for the interpretation of prophecy in *2 Peter 1:20.*

"Know this first, that no prophecy of scripture is of any private interpretation." You don't interpret a single text by itself; you interpret it in the light of the entire Word of God.

"To shew...things" assures us that what John tells us is not dream stuff. There is a hard core of real facts in this book.

"Must" – He says that they must shortly come to pass. The Word must have in it an urgent necessity and absolute certainty.

"Shortly" has a connotation that is very important for us to note.

John tells us that it is the revelation of Jesus Christ. He gave it to His angel. His angel gave it to John and from John, it goes to His servants that they might know what is coming to pass.

CHAPTER 1

The Method of Revelation

Who bare record of the word of God, and of the testimony of Jesus Christ, and of all things that he saw [Rev. 1:2].

"Who bare record," or *"witness,"* of the *"Word of God."* The *"Word of God,"* refers to both Christ and the contents of this book. He is the living Word and when the Written Word reveals Him to us, He is the living Word.

"And of the testimony [witness] of Jesus Christ and of all things that he saw." He was an eyewitness to the visions.

The Beatitude of Bible Study

Blessed is he that readeth, and they that hear the words of this prophecy, and keep those things which are written therein: for the time is at hand [Rev. 1:3].

This verse gives us the beatitude of Bible Study. These are the first seven beatitudes found in the Book of Revelation. This verse says, *"Blessed is he that readeth,"* and that means the reader or the teacher in the church. Both those who read this book and hear it will be blessed. And those who hear it will be blessed. And both the reader and the hearer are to keep those things which are written in the book. The threefold blessing comes from reading, believing, and keeping. Those who go through the Book of Revelation will receive a special blessing.

"For the time is at hand" does not mean that the things which are mentioned at the end of the book are happening in our day, but it does mean that the beginning of the church on the Day of Pentecost began this movement of the Lord Jesus ministry in heaven.

Greetings From John The Writer And From Christ In Heaven

John to the seven churches which are in Asia: Grace be unto you, and peace from him which is, and which was, and which is to come" and from the seven Spirits which are before his throne [Rev. 1:4].

This is a wonderful greeting. *"John to the seven churches which are in Asia,"* encompassed a great deal of what we generally call Asia Minor or modern Turkey. Now let's call attention to the number seven. In this verse, there is the mention of seven churches and seven spirits. The number seven has a religious meaning in the Word of God, which was apparent to the people in John's day but is totally foreign to us in our day. However, in the Word of God, the number seven is prominent. It does not denote perfection, but it does denote completeness. Sometimes completeness is perfection, but not always.

Seven speaks of that which is complete and that which is representative. In a particular way, seven has to do with God's covenant and dealing with Israel. For instance, the sabbath, circumcision, and worship are all hinged around the seventh day.

Seven is the key number of this book. Jesus spoke seven times from the cross, and in the Book of Revelation, the number seven cannot be ignored or considered accidental. In the fourth verse, John writes to the *"seven churches."* Weren't there other churches in Asia?

John was directed to write to only seven certain churches because he was giving the complete history of the church and they were representative churches, as we should see.

"Asia" refers to the provinces, which include Lydia, Myasia, Carcia, and Phrygia. It does not mean the continent of Asia, nor does it include all of Asia minor.

"Grace be unto you and peace." The word grace is Charis, the Greek form of greeting and peace is shalom, the Hebrew form of greeting. Peace flows from grace and grace is the source of all our blessings today. The Book of Revelation reveals the grace of God and also peace. We can have the peace of God in our hearts.

It is *"from him...and from the seven spirits,"* which brings the Trinity before us. The seven spirits refers to the Holy Spirit and probably refers to the seven branches of the lampstand we shall see. Which is and which was and which is to come emphasizes the eternity and immutability of God. Notice the mention of each member of the Trinity.

"Jesus Christ" in the next verse refers to God, the Son. The "seven Spirit" refers to the Holy Spirit and "him which is and which was, and which is to come, refers to God the Father.

And hath made us kings and priests unto God and his Father, to him be glory and dominion forever and ever. Amen [Rev. 1:5-6].

In these two verses, we have the titles given to the Lord Christ, and the interesting thing is that there are seven titles.

1. **Faithful witness:** Jesus Christ is the only trust worthy witness to the fact of this book. The facts are about Him.

2. **First begotten of the dead:** is the firstborn from the dead. Firstborn in the Greek prototoken, which has to do with resurrection. He is the first to rise from the dead, never to die again.

3. The prince [ruler] of the Kings of the earth speaks of His ultimate protection during the Millennium.

4. *"Unto him that loved us"* is actually in the present tense and emphasizes His constant attitude toward His own.

5. *"Washed [blood] is from our sins in his own blood."* The blood of Christ is very important. It is not just a symbol. In the Old Testament, God taught His people that the *"... life of the flesh is in the blood..."* *(Lev. 17:11)*

6. *"And hath made us Kings and priests, [a Kingdom of priests] unto God and this father."* Believers are never called Kings. They are a kingdom of priests and are going to rule with the Lord Jesus.

7. *"To Him the glory and the dominion unto the ages of the ages."* This is emphasizing eternity. *"Amen,"* Christ is the Amen, as we saw in Isaiah. That's a title for Him. Jesus Christ is both the subject and the subject of this book.

Behold, he cometh with clouds; and every eye shall see him, and they also which pierced him: and all kindreds of the earth shall wail because of him. Even so, Amen [Rev. 1:7].

"Beholds, he cometh with clouds" denotes the personal and physical coming of Christ.

"And every eye shall see him" reveals that His coming will be a physical and bodily appearance, and appeals to the eye-gate.

"Every eye shall see him," the emphasis in the Book of Revelation is upon His coming to this earth to establish His kingdom.

"All kindreds of the earth shall wail because of him," This is going to be the reaction of all Christ-rejections. The world will not want to see him.

"Even so, Amen" means *"Yea, faithful."* He is going to do it. He is not going to change His mind about it. He is faithful.

I am Alpha and Omega, the beginning and the ending saith the Lord, which is and which was and which is to come, the Almighty [Rev. 1:8].

"I am Alpha and Omega." This is a remarkable statement in the Greek language. The Alpha and Omega are the first and last letters of the Greek alphabet. From an alphabet, you make words and Jesus Christ is called the *"Word of God"*—the full revelation and intelligent communication of God.

Here the emphasis is on the beginning and the end. In the original Greek, the Omega is not spelled out as in the Alpha. Why? Because Christ is the beginning and the beginning is already completed. But the end is yet to be: One day, He will complete God's program.

"The beginning and the ending" refers to the eternity of the Son and His immutability. When it says that He is the same, it means that in His attributes, He is the same. He has not changed. He is immutable. Since He is the beginning and the ending, He encompasses all time and eternity.

"Saith the Lord" is an affirmation of the deity of the Lord Jesus Christ.

"Which is" that is, at the present time. He is the glorified Christ.

"Which was"—past time, the first coming of Christ as Savior.

"Which is to come"—future time, the second coming of Christ and sovereign over this earth.

The Post-incarnate Christ
In A Glorified Body
Judging His Church

I John, who also am your brother, and companion in tribulation, and in the kingdom and patience of Jesus Christ, was in the isle that is called Patmos, for the word of God, and for the testimony of Jesus Christ [Rev. 1:9].

"I John" is used three times in the Book of Revelation – the other two are at the end of the Book.

"Your brother and companion in tribulation" does not refer to the Great Tribulation. John was in trouble. Domitian (A.D. 96), the Roman emperor, had put him in prison on the Isle of Patmos. You get into trouble when you teach all of the Word of God. John is not referring to the Great Tribulation but to the persecution that was already befalling believers. And *"the Kingdom"* refers to the present state of the Kingdom. By virtue of the new that places a sinner in Christ, He is likewise in the Kingdom of God.

John was given this great vision on the lonely Isle of Patmos. It is a vision of the Post-incarnate Christ in His glorified body. He is judging His Church. In other words, we shall see the Great High Priest in the holy of holies.

CHAPTER 1

Saying, I am Alpha and Omega, the first and the last: and, What thou seest, write in a book, and send it unto the seven churches which are in Asia; unto Ephesus, and unto Smyrna, and unto Pergamos, and unto Thyatira, and unto Sardis, and unto Philadelphia, and Laodicea [Rev, 1:10-11].

The Holy Spirit is here performing His office work. We are beginning to get a vision of the glorified Christ. We are considering Him in His office as the Great High Priest.

"I was in the Spirit," John says. The Holy Spirit was moving upon John and giving him a panoramic picture. This is an appeal to both the eye-gate and the ear-gate.

"On the Lord's day." The meaning of this is controversial — something outstanding. Bible scholars interpret this as being a reference to the Day of the Lord. Although the great theme of Revelation will deal with the Day of the Lord, which is the Tribulation Period and the millennial Kingdom. But John says that he was in the Spirit on the Lord's Day and the Day of the Lord and the Lord's Day are two different things. And that the Lord's Day refers to what we call Sunday.

"I...heard behind me a great voice, as of a Trumpet." Who was it? He will tell us.

And in the midst of the seven candlesticks one like unto the Son of man, clothed with a garment down to the foot, and girt about the paps with a golden girdle [Rev. 1:12-13].

John heard a voice like a war trumpet, and it spoke to him. When the Lord Jesus descends from heaven to remove His church from the earth. He will come with a shout *(1 Thessalonians 4:16)*.

His voice will be like the voice of an arch angel, and His voice will be like a trumpet because it is identified here as just that. But it will be Christ's own voice. He will not need any archangel to help Him raise His own from the dead. The seven golden lampstands remind us of the tabernacle. There it was. One lampstand with seven branches. Here it is seven separate lampstands. These lampstands represents seven separate churches *(v.20)*.

We see the Lord Jesus Christ pictured here as our Great High Priest. His garments are those of the high priest. – check *Exodus 28:2-4.* The garment represent the inherent righteousness of Christ. In Him is no sin and He knew no sin.

Concerning the girdle, Josephus states that the high priests were girded about the breasts. The ordinary custom was to be girded about the loins, but the emphasis here is not on service but on strength. It speaks of His judgment in truth. He is judging the churches: He is judging believers that the light might continue to shine. It is important to see what Christ's present ministry is. It mentions three very definite ministries.

First, there is the intercession of Christ. He is our Great High Priest. He is standing at the golden altar in heaven where He ever lives to make intercession for us (See *Heb. 7:25*).

Second, we have the intervention of Christ. He steps outside of the holy place to the laver. There He washes the feet of those who are His own. There He washes those who have confessed their sins. Christians have sin, and those sins must be confessed in order to have fellowship with Him. He is girded today with the towel and He carries the basin; He intervenes on our behalf.

Third is His ministry of inspection. In the Book of Revelation, we see Him walking in the midst of the lampstands perfecting, His ministry of inspection.

His head and his hairs were white like wool, as white as snow; and his eyes were as a flame of fire; And his feet like unto fine brass, as if they burned in a furnace; and his voice as the sound of many waters [Rev. 1:14-15].

"His head and his hair were white like wool, as white as snow" speaks of His eternal existence, He is the Ancient of Days (see *Daniel 7:9)*. "His eyes were as a flame of fire" speaks of His penetrating insight and eye witness knowledge of the total life of the church, He knows all about you. His feet, like unto fine brass or burnished brass is symbolic of judgement.

That brass or brazen altar outside the tabernacle proper represents Christ's work down here on earth. Here on earth, when He died on the cross, it was there that He is judging those of us who are His own.

The human heart resents criticism. Human nature rebels against judgment being passed upon it. Man likes to be handed a passel of little rules and regulations which he can keep.

"His voice as the sound of many waters is the voice of authority" –the voice that called this universe into existence. That voice that will take His own out of the world to be with Him.

All these figures add to the picture of Christ as our Great High Priest, inspecting and judging His church. The spirit of God will help us see Him in all of His beauty and glory.

And he had in his right hand seven stars: and out of his mouth went a sharp two-edged sword: and his countenance was as the sun shineth in his strength [Rev. 1:16].

"He had in his right hand seven stars" means that He controls this universe.

"Out of his mouth went a sharp two-edged sword" scripture tells us that the sword represents His Word (See *Heb. 4:12)*. God judges by His Word. He judges by it today.

"His countenance was as the sun shineth in his strength." You can't even look at the sun. Do you think you will be able to look at the Creator?

And when I saw him, I fell at his feet as dead. And he laid his right hand upon me, saying unto me, Fear not: I am the first and the last [Rev. 1:17].

John is the disciple who had an easy familiarity with Christ. He reclined upon His bosom in the Upper Room. But when he saw the glorified Christ on the Isle of Patmos, he did not go up to Him and put Him on the back. He fell at His feet as dead! The effect of the vision upon John was nothing short of paralyzing.

But the marvelous thing is that He says, *"Fear not."* This is the greeting of the deity addressing humanity. And he gave four reasons why we should not fear.

1. *"I am the first and last."* This speaks of His deity. He came out of eternity and He moves into eternity (*Ps. 90:2*). The word everlasting means from vanishing point in the past to the vanishing point in the future. He is God. He is first because there were none before Him and He is last, for there are more to follow Him.

I am he that liveth and was dead; and behold. I am alive for evermore, Amen; and have the keys of hell and of death [Rev. 1:18].

2. *"I am he that liveth, and was dead"* – or the living One who became dead. This speaks of His redemptive death and resurrection.

3. *"And. Behold, I am alive for evermore,"* This refers to His present stated. He is not only judging, but He is making intercession for us.

4. *"And have the keys of death and or hades."* The keys speak of authority and power. Jesus has power over death and the grave because of His own death and resurrection. Hades is the Greek word for the unseen world. It can refer to the grave where the body is laid or to the place where the spirit goes.

We can take comfort in the fact that Jesus has the keys of death. He is the One who can relieve us of the terrible fear of death.

Write the things which thou hast seen and the things which are, and the things which shall be hereafter [Rev. 1:19].

1. *"Write the things which thou hast seen."* Up to this point, what had John seen? He had seen the glorified Christ. Let me remind you that this is a Christ-centric book. The glorified Christ is the subject. Fix your eyes on the Lord Jesus Christ. He is the One who was, who is, and will

be. He is the same yesterday, today, and forever. John writes the vision he had of Him.

2. *"The things which are."* What are the things that are? They are the things that pertain to the church. The church things are recorded in chapters 2 and 3.

3. *"The things which shall be hereafter."* (Meta tauta) (Meta tauta).

Interpretation of Seven Stars and Seven Lampstands

The mystery of the seven stars which thou sawest in my right hand, and the seven golden candlesticks. The seven stars are the angels of the seven churches: and the seven candlesticks which thou sawest are the seven churches [Rev. 1:20].

You see, John will make it clear when he is using symbols and he will help us understand what the symbols mean. Otherwise, he is not using symbolic language but is talking about literal things.

"The mystery of the seven stars...and the seven...candlesticks." A mystery in scripture means a sacred secret that has not been revealed before. And His has not been revealed before it was given to John.

The *"seven stars"* are identified as the seven angels. The stars represent authority. In Jude verse 13, apostates are called wandering stars. The word angel literally means messenger and may be either human or angelic beings.

"The seven candlesticks which thou sawest are the seven churches." The English word candlestick should be important since it holds lamps rather than candles. It represents the seven churches of Asia, as we shall see. Then,

in turn, these represent the churches as a whole, the churches in the Body of Christ.

Chapter 2

Theme: *The church in the world*

Christ's Letters to the Church in Ephesus

Unto the angle of the church of Ephesus write; These things saith he that holdeth the seven stars in his right hand, who walketh in the midst of the seven golden candlesticks [Rev. 2:1].

The Lord Jesus Christ speaks to this church in the midst of mass material-ism, degraded animalism, base paganism, and dark heathenish. Notice that Jesus holds in his hand the church. It is under His control. He doesn't have that control now, but He did then.

"He walketh." Literally means that He is walking up and down. We believe that He is still walking up and down in our day and that He is still judging the church.

I know thy works, and thy labour, and bear them which are evil: and thou hast tried them which say they are apostle and are not, and hast found them liars: And hast borne, and hast patience, and for my name's sake hast laboured, and hast not fainted [Rev. 2:2-3].

He has seven words of commendation for this church,

1. *"I know thy works."* We need to understand that He is speaking to believers. The Lord Jesus does not ask that lost world for good works. Christ is talking to His own. After we are saved, He wants to talk to you about good works. He has a lot to say about this subject. In *Eph. 2:8-10*, we read, *"For by grace are ye saved through faith: and that not of yourselves: it is the gift of God: not of work, lest any man should boast."*

2. *"I know...thy labor."* What is the difference between work and labor? The word labor carries a meaning of weariness.

3. *"I know...thy patience."* Patience is a fruit of the Holy Spirit.

4. *"How thou canst not bear them which are evil."* They would not endure evil men.

5. *"Thou hast tried them which say they are apostle and are not, and hast found them liars."* They tested everyone who came to Ephesus, claiming to be an apostle.

6. *"Hast borne...for my name's sake hast laboured."* For His name's sake, they were bearing the cross. They preached Christ. They believed in the virgin birth of Christ. They believed in His Deity. They believed in His sacrificial death and resurrection. And they paid a price for their belief.

7. *"And hast not fainted."* More accurately, it is *"hast not grown weary."*

These seven words of commendation, which the Lord Jesus gave to the local church, at Ephesus also apply to the period of church at Ephesus, the history between Pentecost and A.D. 100, which the Ephesian church represents.

Nevertheless I have somewhat against thee, because thou hast left thy first love [Rev. 2:4].

Now He has one word of condemnation. They had lost that intense and enthusiastic devotion to the person of Christ.

It is difficult for us to sense the state to which the Holy Spirit had brought this church. He had brought the believers in Ephesus into an intimate and personal relationship with Jesus Christ. The world has intruded into the church to such an extent that it is hard for us to conceive of the intense, enthusiastic devotion the early church gave to the person of Christ. The early church first went off the track not in their doctrine but in their personal relationship to Jesus Christ.

This is the reason the Lord Jesus said to the Ephesian believers, *"You are getting away from your first love, your best love."* What is the solution?

Remember therefore from whence thou art fallen, and repent, and do the first works; or else I will come unto thee quickly, and will remove thy candlestick out of his place, except thou repent [Rev. 2:5].

"Remember." That is the first thing they were to do.

"And repent." Believe me, Christians need to repent. We need to break the shell of self-sufficiency.

"Repent!" Repentance means to turn back to Him, and it is the message for believers. But the church needs to repent, which is the message they do not want to hear. Remember, repent, and return unto Him.

"Or else I will come unto thee quickly, and will remove the candlestick out of his place, except thou repent." Christ says that He will remove your lampstand. Christ is still watching the lamps and He doesn't mind trimming the wicks or, even using the snuffer when they refuse to give light.

But this thou hast, that thou hatest the deeds of the Nicolaitans, which I also hate [Rev. 2:6].

Nicolaitans is a compound word. Nikao means *"to conquer,"* and has laos means *"the people."* We get our word laity from that. It is difficult to identify who the Nicolaitans were. (a cult).

The church in Ephesus hated it. Later we will see that the church in Pergamos tolerated it.

He that hath an ear, let him hear what the Spirit saith unto the churches; To him that overcometh will I give to eat of tree of life, which is in the midst of the paradise of God [Rev.2:7].

"He that hath an ear." This is what we call a *"blood tip ear,"* which was the requirement for the Old Testament priests. Not everyone can hear the audible sound, but they missed the message.

"Let him hear what the Spirit saith unto the churches." *"The Spirit"* is the Holy Spirit, the Teacher of the church.

"To him that overcometh" refers to genuine believers and we can overcome only through the blood of the lamb.

"Will I give to eat of the tree of life." You will recall that man was forbidden to eat of the Tree of Life after the fall, as recorded in *Genesis 3:22-24.*

"The paradise of God" means the garden of God. Heaven is primarily a green garden and is not just a place with streets of gold. The church of Ephesus represents the church at its best, the apostolic church.

<u>Christ's Letters to the Church In Smyrna</u>

And unto the angel of the church in Smyrna write; These things saith the first and the last, which was dead, and is alive [Rev 2:8].

Smyrna is the martyr church. The church that suffered martyrdom for Christ. The word Smyrna means *"myrrh"* and carries the meaning of suffering. This verse is a reference to chapter 1, verses 17-18, which says, "And when I saw him. I fell at his feet as dead.

'The first and last" means that there was nothing before Him and there will be nothing to follow Him. He has the final disposition of all things. The persecuted believers need to know that He was the One in charge and that the persecution was in the planning and purpose of God.

"Who became dead and lived" has a real message for martyrs. His experience with death identified Him with the five million who were martyred during this period.

I know thy wisdom and tribulation, and poverty, (but thou art rich) and I know the blasphemy of them which say they are Jews, and are not, but are the synagogue of Satan. Fear none of those things which thou shalt suffer: behold, the devil shall cast some of you into prison, that ye may be tried; and ye shall have tribulation ten days: be thou faithful unto death, and I will give thee a crown of life [Rev. 2:9-10].

There are seven things in this church that the Lord commended.

1. *"Tribulation"* is mentioned first. The word works are not in the best manuscripts. But the church in Smyrna endured much tribulation, and they suffered for the Lord Jesus Christ.

2. *"Poverty"* denotes the lack of material possessions. The early church was made up largely of the poorer classes. *"But thou art rich"* denotes the spiritual wealth of the church – they were blessed with all spiritual blessings. Notice the contrast to the rich church in Laodicea. To that church, He said, *"You think you are rich, but you are really poor and know it."*

3. *"The blasphemy of them which say they are Jews... but are the synagogue of Satan."* The implication is that the Jews in Smyrna who had come to Christ was Jews inwardly as well as outwardly. Speaking of them nationally, the Lord said that their father was *"...Syrian was ready to perish..." (Deut. 26:5).* Smyrna was a city of culture in which many Jews had discarded in their belief in the Old Testament.

4. *"Fear none of those things"* is the encouragement of the Lord to His own in the midst of persecution. This is the second time in this book that the Lord has offered this encouragement.

5. *"The devil [Satan] shall cast some of you into prison."* We are going to look at this fearful creature later on, but Christ labels him as being responsible for the suffering of the saints in Smyrna.

6. *"Ye shall have tribulation ten days."* There were ten intense periods of persecution by ten Roman emperors:

    1. Nero
    2. Domitian
    3. Trajan
    4. Marcus
    5. Severus
    6. Maximinus
    7. Decius
    8. Valerian
    9. Aurelian
    10. Diocletian

7. *"Be thou faithful unto death"* – and they were. They were martyrs for Him. He promises them *"a crown of life."* It's interesting that to them, He is saying that He will give crowns – not crowns of flowers – or of anything else perishable – but crowns that will be eternal.

He that hath an ear, let him hear what the Spirit saith unto the churches; He that overcometh shall not be hurt of the second death [Rev. 2:11].

"He that hath an ear, let him hear what the Spirit saith unto the churches." Is He speaking to you?

"The second death." Dwight L. Moody put it like this: *"He who is born once will die twice; he who is born twice will die once."* *"The second"* is the

death that no believer will experience. The first death concerns the body. The second death concerns the souls and the spirit: it is eternal separation from God.

Christ's Letters to the Church In Pergamum

And to the angel of the church in Pergamos write; These things saith he which hath the sharp sword with two edges [Rev. 2:12].

"To the angel of the church in Pergamos." The church in Pergamum is the representative of church history from the period of approximately A.D. 314 to A.D. 590. Its paganism was unlimited because during this time, the world entered into the church and it began to move away from the person of Christ. This letter was Christ's message to the local church at Pergamum, but it also has the historical significance. This letter was addressed, as were other letters to the angel or messenger of the church, which was probably the one we would call the pastor.

"These things saith he which hath the sharp sword with two edges.," means the Word of God. The Word of God has the answer to man's needs and man's sins, which in Pergamum was false religion. That emphasized religion.

I know thy works and where thou dwellest, even where Satan's seat is: and thou holdest fast my name, and hast not denied my faith, even in those days wherein Antipas was my faithful martyr, who was slain among you, where Satan dwelleth [Rev. 2:13].

"Where thou dwellest." The Lord commends this church for definite things. First, He takes note of their circumstances. He knew that these believers were living in a very difficult place. *"Even where Satan's seat*

[throne] is" reveals that religion was big business in Pergamum and that Satan's headquarters were there.

The reason our Lord said that Satan's throne was in Pergamum was because of the heathen temples. But in John's day, it was Satan's throne.

Now here is another word of commendation to the believers at Pergamum.

"Thou holdest fast my name." They were faithful in their defense of the deity of Christ.

"And hast not denied my faith" refers to the body of true doctrine which is believed by Christians.

Even in those days, Antipas was my faithful martyr. Antipas was a martyr about whom we know not at all. He apparently was the first one at Pergamum and there was a great company of martyrs who followed him. So far, Christ has had only words of commendation for the church at Pergamum.

But I have a few things against thee because thou hast there them that hold the doctrine of Balaam, who taught Balac to cast a stumbling block before the children of Israel, to eat things sacrificed unto idols, and to commit fornication. So has thou also them that hold the doctrine of the Nicolaitans, which thing I hate [Rev. 2:14-15].

The two items for condemnation were the doctrine of Balaam and the doctrine of Nicolaitans. Here is the doctrine of Balaam or teaching of Balaam. Balaam taught Balac how to corrupt Israel by intermarriage with the Moabite women. This introduced into the nation both idolatry and fornication.

During the historical period that the church at Pergamum represents, the uncovenanted world came into the church.

"The doctrine of Nicolaitans." We have seen that the church in Ephesus hated it but here in Pergamum, there were some who were holding that doctrine. Although we don't know exactly what the doctrine was, it probably was a gnostic cult developed by Nicolaus, which advocated license in matters of Christian conduct and apparently a return to religious rituals by clergy, ignoring the priesthood of all believers. Christ says that He hates it!

Repent; or else I will come unto thee quickly, and will fight against them with the sword of my mouth [Rev. 2:16].

"Repent." In other words, *"A change of mind"* (See *1 John 1:9).* If they would not repent, the Lord said He would fight against them with the sword of His mouth, which is the Word of God. We need to be careful to identify with the person of Jesus Christ and to recognize, not the church, but the Word of God as our authority.

He that hath an ear, let him hear what the Spirit saith unto the churches; To him that overcometh will I give to eat of the hidden manna, and will give him a white stone, and in the stone a new name written, which no man knoweth saving he that receiveth it [Rev. 2:17].

"He that hath an ear, let him hear what the Spirit saith unto the churches." This is to you and me today.

"To him that overcometh" is the definition of a genuine Christian. We overcome by the blood of the Lamb. Never are we overcomers, but we

overcome by His shed blood. We know that victory was won by Christ and not by ourselves.

"Hidden manna" speaks of the person and the death of Christ as He is revealed in the Word of God. The believer needs to feed on Christ.—This is a must for spiritual growth.

"I...will give him a white stone, and in the stone a new name written, which no man knoweth saving he that receiveth it." Well, Christ says that He will give each of His own a stone with a new name engraved upon it.

Christ Letter to the Church in Thyatira

And unto the angel of the church in Thyatira write; These things saith the Son of God, who hath his eyes like unto a flame of fire, and his feet are like brass [Rev. 2:18].

The church at Thyatira is representative of Romanism, which takes us into the Dark Ages from A.D. 590 to approximately A.D. 1000. It was a dark period. When you leave Pergamum, we begin to move inland. Thyatira and the remaining three churches are inland.

This picture of the Son of God is in judgment. His eyes are like a flame of fire, searching them out and His feet are like burnished brass, which represents judgment. Christ is judging this church. However, He has words of commendation for this church.

I know thy works, and charity, and service and faith, and thy patience, and thy works and the last to be more than the first [Rev. 2:19].

Christ has six words of commendation for the church of the Dark Age, in which many true believers shared a personal love of Christ which was manifested in works. Works are actually credentials of true believers.

The six words of commendation are:

1. *"Works."* The credential of real believers. *"Adorned the doctrine."*
2. *"Love."* It was a church in which there was love, in spite of the fact that it had gone into ritualism.
3. *"Faith."* Though it is placed after works and love in his instance, it is the main spring that turns the hands of work and love,
4. *"Ministry,"* is service.
5. *"Patience"* is endurance in those days of darkness.
6. *"Thy last works are more than the first."* In this church, works increased rather than diminished. All six virtues are produced within the believers by the Holy Spirit.

There's one charge of condemnation.

Notwithstanding I have a few things against thee, because thou sufferest that woman Jezebel, which calleth herself a prophetess, to teach and to seduce my servants to commit fornication, and to eat things sacrificed unto idols [Rev. 2:20].

Jezebel had brought paganism into the northern Kingdom of Israel. Evidently there was in the local church at Thyatira, a woman who had a reputation as a teacher and prophetess who was the counterpart of Jezebel, the consort of Ahab. And concerning the historical period of the Dark Ages, which the church at Thyatira represents, pagan practices and idolatry were mingled with Christian works and worship. As Jezebel killed Naboth and persecuted God's prophets, so the Roman church instituted the Inquisition during this period.

"Seduce" mean a fundamental departure from the truth, according to Vincent.

Jezebel stands in sharp contrast to Lydia, who came from Thyatira. Jezebel is merely a forerunner of the apostate church.

And I gave her space to repent of her fornication; and she repented not [Rev. 2:21].

"Space" is time. The Lord Jesus Christ has patiently dealt with these false systems for over a thousand years and this false system for over a thousand years and there has been no real change down through the centuries in this system. In Rome boasts that she never changes – Semper idem. Always the same.

Behold, I will cast her into a bed, and them that commit adultery with her into great tribulation, except they repent of their deeds [Rev. 2:22].

"Great tribulation" could refer to the persecution, which Rome is enduring under communism. Or it may mean the Great Tribulation into which the apostate church will go.

"Their deeds" should be translated as her deeds.

And I will kill her children with death; and all the churches shall know that I am he which searcheth the reins and hearts: and I will give unto every one of you according to your works [Rev. 2:23].

CHAPTER 2

"Children" are those who were brought up under this system.

"And I will kill her children with death," is translated by Vincent. *"Let them be part to death with death,"* referring to the second death.

"All the churches" refers to the church of all the ages.

"The reins" literally mean the kidneys and refer to the total psychological makeup- the thoughts, the feeling, the purposes. When He searches the reins and the hearts it means that He searches our entire being.

But unto you I say, and unto the rest in Thyatira, as many as have not this doctrine, and which have not known the depths of Satan, as they speak; I will put upon you none other burden [Rev. 2:24].

The church in Thyatira, we know from history, had a very brief existence because it went down with the city when it was captured by the enemy.

"The depths of Satan" perhaps refers to a gnostic sect known as the Ophites who worshiped the serpent. They made a parody of Paul's words, All heresy boasts of superior spiritual perception, and that's what this group did.

But that which ye have already hold fast till I come [Rev. 2:25].

Obviously, Christ is beginning to say to His church, *"I am coming to take you out, and because of this, you should stand fast for me."*

And he that overcometh, and keepeth my works unto the end, to him will I give power over the nations [Rev. 2:26].

The works of Christ are in contrast to the works of Jezebel. The works of Christ are wrought by the Holy Spirit. We overcome by faith and not by effort.

"I give power over the nations," was explained by Paul when he wrote to the Corinthian believers: *"Do ye not know that the saint shall judge the world...(1 Cor. 6:2)."*

And he shall rule them with a rod of iron; as the vessels of a potter shall they be broken to shivers: even as I received of my Father [Rev. 2:27].

This is a reference to the millennial reign of Christ in which believers are to share.

And I will give him the morning star [Rev. 2:28].

Christ is the bright and morning star (see *Rev. 22:16).* Christ's coming for His own at the Rapture is the hope of the church. *"Looking for that blessed hope, and the glorious appearing of the great God and our Savior Jesus Christ" (Titus 2:13).*

He that hath an ear, let him hear what the Spirit saith unto the churches [Rev. 2:29].

The children of Jezebel will not hear, but the true children of the Lord Jesus will hear, for the Holy Spirit opens the *"Blood-tipped ear."*

Chapter 3

Theme: *The Church in the World – continued*

Christ's Letters to the Church in Sardis

And unto the angel of the church in Sardis write; These things saith he that hath seven stars; I know thy works, that thou hast a name that thou livest, and art dead [Rev. 3:1].

In the panorama of the church, Sardis represents the Protestant church during the period between A.D. 1517 and approximately A.D. 1800.

"These things saith he that hath the seven spirits of God and the seven stars." He presents Himself to the church at Sardis as the One having the seven Spirits of God: that is, He is the One who sent the Holy Spirit into the world.

Sardis represents the Protestant church. The church to this day needs the Spirit of God working in it. We think we need methods. What we really need to do is to get the person of Christ whom only the Holy Spirt can make real and is living to us.

"I know thy works." This is the word of commendation. Remember that the reformation recovered the doctrine of justification by faith and this faith produced works.

"That thou hast a name that thou livest and art dead." Protestantism today, as a whole, has a name that it lives, but it is dead.

Many Protestant Churches today are just going through the form.

"Thou hast a name that thou livest, and art dead." This is a frightful condemnation and it is a picture of Protestantism today.

We need to recognize that all of the truth was not recovered by the reformation. For example, we believe that the doctrine of eschatology, prophecy, is just now being developed in our own day.

Be watchful, and strengthen the things which remain, that are ready to die: for I have not found thy works perfect before God [Rev. 3:2].

This is the second word of condemnation and a word of warning that had a particular meaning in Sardis. The Lord says to this church at Sardis: *"You wake up and watch out!"* Because of the two occasions in their history when they had been caught napping. He says to the church, *"Don't you go to sleep."*

Protestantism, as a whole, has turned away from looking for the coming of Jesus Christ, and they have built up these systems that certain things must be fulfilled before He can come.

In view of the fact that the Rapture could take place at any moment, the church is to be alert. *"Looking for that blessed hope..." Titus 2:13.* The Lord Jesus is saying to Protestantism that they are constantly to be on the alert.

"For I have not found thy works perfect before God." Protestantism did recover the authority of the Word of God, the total depravity of man, and justification by faith, but there are many other things that they did not recover. The reformation was not a return to the apostolic church.

Remember therefore how thou hast received and heard, and hold fast, and repent, If therefore thou shalt not watch, I will come on thee as a thief and thou shalt not know what hour I will come upon thee [Rev. 3:3].

"Remember therefore how thou hast received and heard, and hold fast, and repent." The idea is that they were to hold fast to these things because they were about to die. The great truths which were recovered in the reformation are being lost. For instance, the Protestant church, by and large, has lost the authority of the Word of God. Rather than holding to the doctrine of the total depravity of man, many of our conservative churches are improving and using cosmetics on the carnal nature, thinking that somehow or another, you can get up a few little rules and regulations which are going to enable you to live the Christian life. Also, the great doctrine of justification by faith has been pretty much abandoned, and a legalistic message is given that you have to do something in order to be saved. These are the things that characterized Protestantism today: It is very far from its original position.

"If therefore thou shalt not watch, I will come on thee as a thief, and thou shalt not know what hour I will come upon thee."

The Lord says to the church at Sardis, *"Don't you go to sleep. Wake up and watch out."* He could come at any moment. The people of Sardis did not know when the enemy was coming, and we don't know when the Lord Jesus is coming.

Thou hast a few names even in Sardis which have not defiled their garments; and they shall walk with me in white: for they are worthy [Rev. 3:4].

In Israel it was never the corporate body of the total national life but always a remnant that was true to God.

He that overcometh, the same shall be clothed in white raiment; and I will not blot out his name out of the book of life, but I will confess his name before my Father, and before his angels [Rev. 3:5].

"He that overcometh." The one who overcomes by the blood of Christ, of course, never does it because of his own strength, cleverness, or ability. The whole thought is simply that it was amazing that anyone in Sardis would be saved but that there were some whose names He said would not be blotted out of the Book of Life. He didn't say that anybody had been blotted out. He just said that even in Sardis there would be some saved. The important thing is whether or not your name is written in the Lamb's Book of Life. We don't believe that after you are saved you would even be able to lose that salvation.

He that hath an ear, let him hear what the Spirit saith unto the churches [Rev. 3:6].

Again, this is the blood-tipped ear that needs to hear the voice of the Spirit speaking through the Word of God, the message of Christ to His church today.

CHAPTER 3

Christ's Letter to the Church In Philadelphia

And to the angel of the church in Philadelphia write; These things saith he that is holy, he that is true, he that hath the key of David, he that openeth, and no man shutteth; and shutteth, and no man openeth [Rev. 3:7].

The church in Philadelphia represents the revived church dating from approximately the beginning of the nineteenth century to the Rapture. This is the church that has turned back to the Word of God. This church and Smyrna, and our Lord had no word of condemnation. Why? Because it had turned to the Word of God. It's interesting that the two churches that He did not condemn that the places are still in existence.

"And to the angel of the church in Philadelphia write." The angel is the human messenger, the pastor: if you will of the church. This is the Lord's method in all these churches.

"These things saith he that is holy, he that is true, he that hath the key of David, he that openeth, and no man shutteth: and shutteth, and no man openeth," in each of these messages, the Lord always draws something from the vision of Himself as the glorified Christ, our Great High Priest.

"He that is true." John 14:6 tells us, *"...I am the way, the truth and the life..."* True means *"genuine"* with an added note of perfection and completeness. Moses did not give the true bread: Christ is the true bread (see *John 6:32-35*).

"He that hath the key of David." This is different from the keys of hades and death, which we saw in chapter 1, verse 18. This speaks of His regal claims as the ruler of this universe (see *Luke 1:32-33*). He will sit on the

throne of David in the Millennium, but today He is sovereign, sitting at His Fathers' right hand, waiting for His enemies to be made His footstool.

"He that openeth, and no man shutteth; and shutteth, and no man openeth." He is the One today, who is able to open and to close, and because of that He is comfort to us. (See *Matt. 28:18-20*).

I know thy works: behold, I have set before thee an open door; and no man can shut it: for thou hast kept my word, and hast not denied my name [Rev. 3:8].

The church in Philadelphia was the one that was true to the Word of God. The Lord commends the Philadelphian church on seven counts.

1. *"I know thy works."* The Lord Jesus is looking for fruit: He is looking for works in the lives of believers. (see *Eph. 2:8-10; James 2:18*). *"Works are not works of law, but works of faith."* Calvin said, *"Faith alone saves, but faith that saves is not alone. Saving faith produces works."*

2. *"Behold, I have set before thee an open door and no man can shut it."* This could be a door to the joy of the Lord or to a knowledge of the scriptures. We believe its of the knowledge of Scriptures:

3. *"For thou hast a little strength [dunamin]."* Dunamin is the Greek word for which we get our English word dynamite. He says, *"You have a little power."*

4. *"And hast kept my word."* In a day when there was a denial of the inspiration of the Scriptures, this church believed the Bible to be the authoritative, inspired Word of God.

5. *"And hast not denied my name."* In a day when the deity of Christ is blatantly denied by the seminary, and pulpit, here is a group of believers who have remained true to Him by proclaiming the God-man and His substitutionary death for sinners.

Behold, I will make them of the synagogue of Satan, which say they are Jews, and are not, but do lie; behold, I will make them to come and worship before thy feet, and to know that I have loved thee [Rev. 3:9].

The remnant of Israel which was being saved had left the synagogue by this time. They had given up the Law as a means of salvation and sanctification. Those who continued in the synagogue were now in a false religion. (*Rom. 9:6)-* they were no longer true Jews. He considered the true Israelite to be the one who had turned to Christ.

6. *"Behold, I will make them to come and worship before thy feet, and to know that I have loved thee."* The Lord Jesus says that He will make the enemies of the Philadelphian church to know that He loves this church. This is His sixth point of commendation.

Because thou hast kept the word of my patience, I also will keep thee from the hour of temptation, which shall come upon all the world, to try them that dwell upon the earth [Rev. 3:10].

This last commendation is that this church kept the Word of Christ in patience. This is evidently the patient waiting for the coming of Christ for His own. (See *2 Thess. 3:5*).

"Because thou hast kept the word of my patience." God today is still patient with a world that has rejected His Word. The Philadelphian church is the church that believed in the Word of God.

"I also will keep thee from the hour of temptation, which shall come upon all the world, to try them that dwell upon the earth." Christ's final word of commendation of encouragement to His church is that it will not pass through the Great Tribulation. The church is to be removed from the world (See *1 Thess. 4:13-18*), which is its comfort and hope (see *Titus 2:13*).

"The hour of temptation" is definitely a reference to the Great Tribulation – it's world-wide. This is the period that He says is coming upon all the world to test those that are upon the earth.

"I will also keep thee from the hour of temptation." He says that He will keep them not only from that awful holocaust that is coming on this earth, that period of judgement, but also from the hour of temptation. This is the church which will go out at the time of the rapture. Now the church of Laodicea, as we shall see, is an organization that will continue on in the world, although the Lord gives a marvelous invitation to it, and many will turn to Christ and be taken out at the time of the rapture. But there is a church that goes through the Great Tribulation Period and that is the apostate church, the church or Laodicea.

Behold, I come quickly: hold that fast which thou hast, that no man take thy crown [Rev. 3:11].

"Behold, I come quickly." "Quickly" does not mean soon. Rather, it has the idea of suddenness and an air of expectation: that is, He will come at a time they know not. It does not mean He is coming immediately, but His coming will be sudden. This is the promise that is the hope of the church. Let us say again that the Philadelphian church represents the revived church, the church that has returned to the Word of God.

Him that overcometh will I make a pillar in the temple of my God, and he shall go no more out: and I will write upon him the name of my God, and the name of the city of my God, which is new Jerusalem, which cometh down out of heaven from my God: and I will write upon him my new name [Rev. 3:12].

There are two pillars in Philadelphia today. One is that of the Byzantine church. But there is also a pillar on the side of the hill, hidden among those cedar and laurel trees. That pillar is all that remains of the city of John's day.

"Him that overcometh will I make a pillar in the temple of my God." The church down here was destroyed, but the permanent pillar is up yonder.

"And I will write upon him the name of my God, and the name of the city of my God, which is the new Jerusalem which cometh down out of heaven from my God; and I will write upon him my new name." This is the passport and. Visa of the believer, which will enable him, as a citizen of heaven, to pass freely upon this earth or anywhere in God's universe.

"I will write upon him my name." This is His name. We do not have a new name. Rather, He is saying that He has a new name for Himself that He will give to us. This new name is a personal relationship we will have with Him.

He that hath an ear, let him hear what the Spirit saith unto the churches [Rev. 3:13].

The Lord has a message to each of these churches. It applied to that local church, but also to us today.

Christ's Letter to the Church In Laodicea

And unto the angel of the church of the Laodiceans write; These things saith the Amen, the faithful and true witness, the beginning of the creation of God [Rev.3:14].

The letter of Christ to the church in Laodicea is the last of the seven letters. This is the only place in Scripture where Amen is a proper name and it is the name of Christ. *Isaiah 65:16* should read, *"the God of the amen."* In *Isaiah 7:9*, the word believer is amen. In *2 Corinthians 1:20*, we read, *"For all the promises of God in him are yea, and in him amen, unto the glory of God by us."* The Lord Jesus is the Amen. He has the last word. He is the Alpha and the Omega. He is the One who is going to fulfill all the promises of God, and He lets the Laodiceans know this because this is the church that has rejected the deity of Christ. The word Amen is the only thing that He draws out of the vision of Himself that we had in the first chapter.

"The faithful and true witness." This reveals that the Lord Jesus Christ alone is the One who will reveal all and tell all. This is the day when it is very difficult to hear the truth. Well. There is one who is the faithful and true witness even in the days of apostasy. You can not believe the church in many instances today: the liberal church has no message for this hour.

"The beginning of the creation of God" means that He is the creator. The Lord Jesus is "the beginning of the creation of God."

I know thy works, that thou art neither cold nor hot: I would thou wert cold or hot. So then because thou art lukewarm, and neither cold nor hot, I will spue thee out of my mouth [Rev. 3:15-16].

Now with the other churches whom the Lord Jesus said, *"I know thy works."* He meant good works; He was commending them for good works. But the Lord Jesus has no word of commendation for this church. All is condemnation here. Even the "work" here are not good works. They are evil works.

"That thou are neither cold nor hot: I would thou were cold or hot." This had a background and a local meaning for the people in that day. Now the Laodiceans built an aqueduct to bring that cold water down from the mountains. When it felt it was ice cold, but when it reached Laodicea, it was lukewarm, and lukewarm water is not good.

Now in the valley where the Lycus River joins the Maeander River, there are hot springs. Now when they would take this hot water up. It no longer was hot. It had become lukewarm. When the Lord Jesus said to the Laodicean church, *"You are neither cold nor hot."* They knew exactly what He was talking about. A cold church actually means a church that has denied every cardinal doctrine of the faith.

Hot speaks of those with real spiritual fervor and passion like the Christians in Ephesus although they were even then getting away from their best love. But the Laodicean church was neither hot nor cold – just lukewarm. This is a picture of many Churches today in the great denomination that have departed from the faith. Many of these churches attempt to maintain a middle of the road position.

"Thou hast a name that thou livest, and art dead" (v.1) *"Having a form of godliness but denying the power thereof"* from such turn away (*2 Tim. 3:5*). You're professed Christians. You say you love Me. You say, but don't mean it.

This is a heart searching message for this hour because we are living in the time of the Laodicean church and of the Philadelphian church. Both of them are side by side and there is a great bifurcation in Christianity today. It's not in denominations, and it's not Romanism and Protestantism. The great bifurcation (divide) consists of those who believe the Word of God and follow it, love it, obey it, and those who reject it. That is the line of division today.

Because they sayest, I am rich. And increased with goods. And have need of nothing; and knowest not that thou art wretched, and miserable. And poor, and blind, and naked [Rev. 3:17].

"Because thou sayest I am rich." The city of Laodicea was a rich city. Laodicea and Sardis were probably two of the riches cities in that entire area of this time.

"Because thou sayest I am rich and increased with good, and have need of nothing." They believed that the dollar was the answer to every problem of life.

The Laodicean church made it's boast of material possessions. Conversely, the church in Smyrna was poor in material things. It was the church of slaves and poor folk. The present day church boast of large memberships, prominent people, huge attendance, generous giving and ornate buildings. This would indicate the possibility of a church on fire for God.

Worldly wealth is the measuring rod for the modern church. Spiritual values have been lost sight of or are entirely ignored.

On the spiritual side of the ledger, the Laodicean church is *"the wretched one."* It's worse off than any of the seven churches. It is to be pitied because it is spiritually poverty stricken. In it is no study of the Word, no love of Christ, and no witnessing of His saving grace: yet it is blind to its own true condition. We are living in the Laodicean period today and the church is failing to witness to the saving grace of God.

I counsel thee to buy of me gold tried in the fire, that thou mayest be rich; and white raiment, that thou mayest be clothed, and that the shame of thy nakedness do not appear; and anoint thine eyes with eye-salve, that thou mayest see [Rev. 3:18].

"I counsel thee to buy of me gold tried in the fire, that thou mayest be rich." – This is the precious blood of Christ.

"And white raiment, that thou mayest be clothed, and that shame of thy nakedness do not appear" – this speaks of the righteousness of Christ.

"And anoint thine eyes with eye-salve, that thou mayest see." – This speaks of the Holy Spirit who opens the eyes of the believers. This admonition was very meaningful to the church at Laodicea.

As many as I love, I rebuke and chasten: be zealous therefore, and repent [Rev.3:19].

This word zealous means *"to be hot."* This is His last message to the church. He says. *"Be zealous."* Be hot. Get on fire for God. He ordered this church to forsake it's lukewarm state and He says, *"Repent."* This church needs repentance more than all the others. And the message or repentance is for the contemporary church, that you will not be popular if you preach that. It is not too late even for those in this church to turn to Christ. *"As many as I love, I rebuke and chasten: be zealous therefore, and repent."*

Behold. I stand at the door. And knock: if any man hear my voice, and open the door, I will come in to him, and will sup with him, and he with me [Rev.3:20].

This is a picture of the Lord Jesus at the heart's door of the sinner. *"I will come in to him, and will sup with him. And he with me."* This speaks of fellowship of feeding on the Word of God and of coming to know Jesus Christ better.

To him that overcometh will I grant to sit with me on my throne, even as I also overcame, and am set down with my Father in his throne [Rev. 3:21].

Again, I called attention to the fact that when the Lord Jesus speaks of *"His relationship with the Father..."* (*John 20:17*) – not our Father – because the relationship is always different with Him.

The Lord Jesus is preparing us for the next scene that will be coming up when He says, *"and am set down with my Father in his throne."* This is the picture that we are going to see in the chapter which follow.

He that hath an ear, let him hear what the Spirit saith unto the churches [Rev. 3:22].

This is a special message from the Lord Jesus to all the churches for which you need the blood-tipped ear to hear. This is the reason that you and I must be very careful in our study of the Word of God, that we not run ahead of the Spirit of God, but that we let Him be our teacher. If you have a blood tipped ear He wants you to hear what He has to say, Only the Spirit of God can make the Word of God real to you. This concludes the message to these seven churches. And there is also a message in each of these churches for you and me today.

To the church at Ephesus: Warning of the danger of getting away from the best love that getting away from a personal and loving relationship with Christ Jesus.

To the church at Smyrna: The Lord Jesus told them not to fear suffering. We don't want to pay a price for serving the Lord Jesus and yet that is His method.

To the church in Pergamum: There is a great danger in wrong doctrine, doctrine of Balaam, and doctrine of Nicolaitans.

To the church in Thyatira: The "new morality" is a grave danger for us today.

To the church in Sardis: the danger of spiritual darkness.

To the church in Philadelphia: no condemnation but a great danger of drifting away.

To the church in Laodicea: They were lukewarm. Neither cold nor hot. This is the apostate church that professes to be Christian but lacks reality. But even to this church He issues a final call to repentance and invitation to come to Himself.

Chapter 4

Theme: *The church in Heaven with Christ*

The Throne of God

After this I looked, and behold, a door was opened in heaven: and the first voice which I heard was as it were of a trumpet talking with me; which said, Come up hither, and I will shew thee things which must be hereafter [Rev.4:1].

Here Christ is viewed here in His threefold office of Prophet, Priest, and King. He is worshipped as God because He is God.

"After these things" (meta tauta) is used twice here; It both opens and closes the verse.

"I saw" – that is the eye-gate. *"I heard"* – that is the ear-gate.

Heaven is a real place. There is a lot of reality there, and we ought not to get uptight over this scene that is now before us. We need to handle it in a normal way.

"I saw, and behold a door set open in heaven." This is one of the four open doors in the Book of Revelation.

1. In chapter 3, verse 8, speaking to the church in Philadelphia, the Lord Jesus says, I have set before thee an open door. It seems that this refers to a door of opportunity for giving out the Word of God.

2. The open door of invitation and identification with Christ is in Chapter 3, verse 20. *"Behold, I stand at the door and knock: if any man hear my voice, and open the door, I will come in to him, and will sup with him, and he with me."* That door is the door to your heart.

3. We have an open door here in verse 1, which is the way to God through Christ.

4. In chapter 19, verse 11, we see a door opened in heaven again. That is the open door through which Christ will come at His second coming. He comes out at the end of the Great Tribulation to put down all of the unrighteousness and rebellion against God and to establish His Kingdom.

"Come up hither" is heaven's invitation to John, and it is an invitation to all the fellowship that knows Christ as Savior.

John is saying in effect, *"We heard it, we saw it, and we declare it unto you. I am letting you know this so that you can have fellowship also, and one of these days, you will be going up through that open door."*

"And the first voice which I heard was a voice as a trumpet speaking with me." This is the sound that calls the church to meet Christ in the air. And whose voice is it? It is the voice of Christ. This introduces us to one of the

simple symbols which occurs frequently from here on in the Revelation. That it is a symbol is evident – a trumpet does not speak.

The trumpet never talks. The voice of Christ is like a trumpet and this is the voice that Paul wrote of in 1 Thessalonians 4:16-17: This is a definite statement concerning the rapture. When anyone tells you that the word rapture is not in the Bible, remember that the Greek word for *"caught up"* is harpazo; it means "caught up, raptured, or snatched up."

"Come up hither and I will show thee the things which must come to pass after these things." After what things? After the church has completed its earthly rein and is caught up.

And immediately I was in the spirit; and behold, a throne was set in heaven, and one sat on the throne [Rev 4:2].

"At once (straight way)" denotes the brevity of time, which is one of the characteristics of the rapture. Paul said that we are to be caught up *"in a moment, in the twinkling of an eye"* (see *1 Cor. 15:51-52*). A twinkling of an eye is pretty brief.

"I found myself in the Spirit." In other words, the Holy Spirit is still guiding John into now truth and is showing him things to come (see *John 16:13).*

"And behold, a throne is set in heaven, and one sitting on the throne." The throne was already there, but John now sees it for the first time. Our attention is now directed to the center of attraction. The throne represents the universal sovereignty and rulership of God. It means that He is in control. The general headquarters of this universe is in heaven, not D.C., not London or Moscow, or any place down here. The throne of grace now becomes a throne of judgment.

And he that sat was to look upon like a jasper and a sardine stone: and there was a rainbow round about the throne, in sight like unto an emerald [Rev. 4:3].

All that we see here is color, beautiful colors like a precious stone. We do not get a picture of God at all – He has never been photographed. Our attention is directed to the One who is seated on the throne. Although He is God the Father, we should understand this to be the throne of the triune God. Nevertheless, the three persons of the Trinity are distinguished.

1. God the Holy Spirit in verses 2 and 5:
2. God the Father here in verse 3; and
3. God the Son in verse 5 of chapter 5.

What we have before us here is the Trinity upon the throne. John could distinguish no form or a person on the throne, only the brilliance and brightness of the precious stone.

"And he that sat was to look upon like a jasper." The jasper stone was the last stone identified in the breast plate of the high priest (see *Exodus 28:20*). It was first in the foundation of the New Jerusalem and also the first seen in the wall of the New Jerusalem (See *Rev. 21:18-19*). It was a many colored stone with purple predominating. It was in the breastplate of the high priest of Israel, representing little Benjamin, whom Jacob called, *"the Son of my right hand!"* Perhaps this speaks of Christ as He ascended and took His place at the right hand of the Father.

The *"Sardine Stone"* in the sixth stone in the foundation of the New Jerusalem (see *Rev. 21:20*). In color, it was a fiery red. The sardine stone was the first stone in the breastplate of the high priest, representing the tribe of

Reuben, the first born of Jacob. And Christ is the Son of God, the firstborn from the dead.

"Rainbow" is the Greek word iris, which can also mean halo.

While the rainbow is polychrome, here it is emerald, which is green (see *Ezek. 1:28)*. It appears here before the judgement of the Great Tribulation as a reminder that a flood will not be used in judgement. Green is the color of the earth. The suggestion here is that of the prophet Habakkuk *"...in wrath remember mercy" (Hab. 3:2)*.

The Twenty-Four Elders

And round about the throne were four and twenty seats: and upon the seats I saw four and twenty elders sitting, clothed in white raiment; and they had on their heads crown of golds [Rev. 4:4].

There has been a great deal of speculation as to who these elders are. The Greek word for *"elders"* is presbuteros. By the way, it is where the word presbyterian comes from. Their role was clearly understood by the people in John's day. These twenty-four elders stand for the total church from Pentecost to the Rapture.

"White raiment" is the righteousness of Christ (see *2 Cor. 5:21)*.

"Crown of gold" indicates that the church will rule with Christ (see *1 Cor. 6:3)*. Crowns are also given as rewards (see *2 Tim. 4:8, James 1:12, 1 Peter 5:4)* when the bema judgment, the judgment seat of Christ takes place.

And out of the throne proceeded lightnings and thundering and voices: and there were seven lamps of fire burning before the throne, which are the seven Spirits of God [Rev. 4:5].

The tense here is the present tense; it should be proceed, not proceeded.

"Lightnings and thunderings" always precede a storm in the Midwest and generally indicate the intensity of the storm. The meaning here is that judgment is coming.

"And voices" indicates that it is not a haphazard judgment, but is directed by the One on the throne.

"The seven Spirits of God" is a clear reference to the Holy Spirit.

The Four Living Creatures

And before the throne there was a sea of glass like unto crystal: and in the midst of the throne, and round about the throne, were four beasts full of eyes before and behind [Rev. 4:6].

"A sea of glass" denotes its appearance and not the material of which it is made. This sea is before the throne of God and is another indication that the emphasis is not on mercy but on judgment. This sea represents the holiness and righteousness of God (see *Matt. 5:8; Heb. 12:14).*

This placid sea indicates the position of rest to which the church has come. No longer is she the victim of the storms of life. No longer is she out there on the tossing sea.

"Four beasts" are literally *"four living creatures."* The Greek word is zoa, from which we get our English word zoo. It doesn't mean a wild beast as we might think. We will have a wild beast when we get to chapter 13, but that is a different word and a different type of beast.

This is just a living creature. The emphasis is not upon the bestial but upon the vital, upon the fact that they are living.

"Four beasts full of eyes before and behind." This speaks of their alertness and awareness. They resemble both the cherubim of *Ezekiel 1:5-10; 10-20;* and the seraphim of *Isaiah 6:2-3.*

And the first beast was like a lion, and the second beast like a calf, and the third beast had a face like a man, and the fourth beast was like a flying eagle [Rev 4:7].

The first living creature was like a lion and the first Gospel represents the Lord Jesus as the King. Everything He does in the Gospel of Matthew, He does as the King. Remember that God said that the tribe of Judah was like a lion, that the King, the Ruler would come from that tribe.

The second living creature is like a calf [ox]. This is the beast of burden, the servant animal domesticated. In the Gospel of Mark, Christ in presented as the Servant. The Gospel of Mark presents Christ as the Servant.

The third living creature had a face like a man. The third Gospel, the Gospel of Luke, presents the Lord Jesus as the Son of Man. It is His humanity that is emphasized.

The fourth living creature was like a flying eagle. He communicates the deity of Christ as seen in the Gospel of John.

These living creatures also represent the animal world, as suggested by Godet. The lion represents wild beasts, the calf represents domesticated beasts, the eagle represents birds, and man is the head of all creation. Note that there is no mention of fish. In the new heaven and the new earth, there will be no more sea, and since there is no sea, you will not need any fish. Nor will there be reptiles. The serpent will not be there to introduce sin as he did at the beginning.

And the four beasts had each of them six wings about him; and they were full of eyes within: and they rest not day and night, saying, Holy, holy, holy, Lord God almighty which was, and is, and is to come [Rev. 4:8].

These six wings correspond to the seraphim of *Isaiah 6:2*. Instead of had, it should be having – this is the present tense. This is where the action is and this is taking place. That which they say repeatedly is *"Holy, holy, holy, Lord God Almighty."* This is the same refrain as that of the seraphim in *Isaiah 6:3.*

"Which was, and is, and is to come" refers to Christ. He identified Himself at the very beginning of this book in just that way: *"I am Alpha and Omega, the beginning and the ending saith the Lord. Which is, and which was and which is to come, the Almighty" Rev 1:8.* He identified for us, and therefore we don't need to speculate.

And when those beasts give glory and honour and thanks to him that sat on the throne, who liveth for ever and ever, The four and twenty elders fall down before him that sat on the throne, and worship him that liveth for ever an ever, and cast their crowns before the throne, saying, Thou art worthy, O Lord, to receive glory and honour and power: for thou hast created all things, and for thy pleasure they are and were created [Rev. 4:9-11].

This is the first great worship scene that we see in heaven. When should be whensoever, indicating that this is a continual act of worship. In other words, praise and adoration are the eternal activity of God's creatures in heaven.

The creature worships the Creator as the triune God: *"Holy, holy, holy."* Worship is the activity of heaven.

"And cast their crowns before the throne." The crowns of the church are laid at Jesus' feet as an act of submission and worship.

"For thou hast created all things." The living creatures give glory and honor and thanks to Him who sits on the throne. They worship Him for His attributes because He is who He is! However, the four and twenty elders who represent the church worshipped Him because of His attributes and what He has done. Here they worship Him as Creator – *"thou hast created all things and for thy pleasure they are and were created."* In other words, the church comes out of this little earth which is God's creation and they join in the worship because He created this earth *(Genesis 1:1)*.

"And for thy pleasure they are and were created." For thy pleasure is more accurately translated *"because of thy will."*

The reason that God created this earth and that things are as they are is because it was in His plan and purpose. We are glad that we are in the plans and purpose of God. We worship Him because of that.

Chapter 5

Theme: *The church in heaven with Christ – continued*

The Book with Seven Seals

And I saw in the right hand of him that sat on the throne a book written within and on the backside, sealed with seven seals [Rev. 5:1].

"I saw" – John witnesses these events; this is something that he sees. John is seeing and he is hearing. The Word of God should grasp and lay hold of all of our senses, even our taste and smell! God the Father holds here in His hands a scroll which is rolled tightly and sealed closely with seven seals.

This suggests that what is being handed over to the Lord Jesus (we will see it handed over to Him) is the title deed to this world in which we live. He created it. He redeemed it and it belongs to Him.

The Old Covenant which God had made with Israel depended upon man. There wasn't anything wrong with the Ten Commandments or with the Law that God gave. The problem was with man. The problem was not the fruit on the tree, but the pear (pair) on the ground. The New Covenant depends upon the power of the throne of God. It depends upon the Lord Jesus Christ.

And I saw a strong angel proclaiming with a loud voice, Who is worthy to open the book, and to loose the seals thereof? [Rev. 5:2].

Who has the right and title to this world? Who rule it? Who can establish justice and righteousness?

"A strong angel" means a powerful angel. He has *"a loud voice."* This is speaking now of power, that which is needed to make this covenant effective.

And no man in heaven, nor in earth neither under the earth, was able to open the book, neither to look thereon [Rev. 5:3].

No man of Adam's line has a right to open the book and to take charge of this earth. Adam lost dominion through sin. Moses was the lawgiver, but he was a lawbreaker. David and his line failed. None of Adam's lines qualifies. There is none today. The Ruler must be a Redeemer, the Sovereign must be a Savior of mankind, and Jesus Christ is the only One.

And I wept much, because no man was found worthy to open and to read the book, neither to look thereon [Rev. 5:4].

John is disturbed by this a great deal. This man had a real passion for prophecy. He had a holy affection and a pious curiosity. He wanted to look into the things that even angels cannot look into. The Revelation was written with tears. Is the earth to continue in sin and sorrow? Is there no future for the earth? Is no one competent to rule this earth? John is overwhelmed by the possibility that there may be no one.

CHAPTER 5

And one of the elders saith unto me, Weep not: behold, the Lion of the tribe of Juda, the Root of David, hath prevailed to open the book, and to loose the seven seals thereof [Rev. 5:5].

Evidently, anyone of the elders could have answered. They had spiritual illumination. The Lord Jesus Christ is the only One with the right and title to this earth. He not only redeemed us, but He also redeemed the earth. He is identified in this section in all His ministries that relate to the earth.

"The Lion of the tribe of Juda," identifies Him, of course, with the tribe of Judah of the people of Israel. When old Jacob was dying, he called his twelve sons around him and this is the prophecy he gave concerning Judah:

"Judah is a lion whelp" from the prey my son thou art gone up. *"He stooped down he couched as a lion, and as an old lion; who shall rouse him up? The scepter shall not depart from Judah, until Shiloh come; and unto him shall the gathering of the people be" (Gen. 49:9-10).*

The Lord Jesus is the Lion of the tribe of Judah. He is also *"the Root of David."* In *2 Samuel 7.* That great chapter of God's covenant with David.

The Lord Jesus Christ has the right to be Ruler as He is the fulfillment of the prophecies made in the Old Testament relative to the future of the world. These prophecies will be fulfilled at His Second coming to the earth to establish His Kingdom.

And beheld, and, lo, in the midst of the throne and of the four beasts, and in the midst of the elders, stood a Lamb as it had been slain, having seven horns and seven eyes, which are the seven Spirits of God sent forth into all the earth [Rev. 5:6].

John is still a spectator in this scene. He says, *"I beheld, I saw this."*

"A Lamb" is the word in the diminutive: literally, it means a little lamb. This denotes it's gentleness and it's a wiliness to be sacrificed. Christ was led as a lamb to the slaughter, and He did not open His mouth at all (see *Isa. 53:7*). He was the Lamb of God who taketh away the sin of the world (see *John 1:29*).

"As it had been slain" indicates the redemptive and vicarious, substitutionary death of Christ. The emphasis is on the fact that He was slain with violence.

"Stood" should rather be *"standing."* This speaks of His resurrection. He is no longer seated at the right hand of God. He is moving now, and He is moving to power. He is coming to this earth. The judgement of the Tribulation is about to strike the earth. The winds are already blowing on the earth.

"In the midst of the throne" indicates that He is before the throne and ready to act as the righteous Judge.

"Seven horns" denotes complete power. A horn speaks of power (see *Dan. 7-8*). He is omnipotent.

"Seven eyes" denotes complete knowledge. He is omniscient. He is the omnipotent and omniscient God. He moves in fullness of the Spirit, who is the Spirit of wisdom and understanding. The Lord Jesus Christ is a Lion and a Lamb. The lion character refers to His second coming. The lamb character refers to this first coming.

The lion is symbolic of His majesty; the lamb is symbolic of His meekness.

As a lion He is a Sovereign.
As a lamb He is a Savior.
As a lion He is a Judge.
As a lamb He is judged.
The lion represents the government of God. The lamb represents the grace of God.

And he came and took the book out of the right hand of him that sat upon the throne [Rev. 5:7].

"Took" is correctly *"hath taken."* The Lord Jesus moves to the throne through the Tribulation Period. He judges the world in righteousness before He reigns in righteousness. He is no longer the intercessor of the church, for the church is now with Him. He is beginning to act as Judge. The movement here is important.

And when he had taken the book, the four beasts and four and twenty elders fell down before the Lamb, having every one of them harps, and golden vials full of odours, which are the prayers of saints [Rev. 5:8].

"When he had taken [took] the book" is in the aorist tense, meaning completed actions. This is the great movement of all creation, and the Lord Jesus takes over now. Notice the worship of the Lamb by the four living creatures and the twenty four elders.

"Harps" denotes praise. The elders do not play on the harps: they are just a token of praise to God. The twenty four elders act as priests. Only the church is a priesthood of believers in heaven.

The *"vials full of odours"* is more accurately *"bowls full of incense."* These are identified as *"the prayers of saints."* Obviously, the elders represent the Body of Christ, which is called the church and they are the priesthood.

And they sung a new song, saying, Thou art worthy to take the book, and to open the seals thereof: for thou wast slain, and hast redeemed us to God by thy blood out of every kindred, and tongue, and people, and nation; And hast made us unto our God kings and priests: and we shall reign on the earth [Rev. 5:9-10].

"They" indicates that both the living creatures and the elders sing this song. The angelic hast join the church in praise.

"Sing" (present tense) denoted the continuation of praise. Praise is directed to the Lamb with the book. He is praised now as the Redeemer of man in all ages and races.

The *"new song"* is the song of redemption. The old song is the song of creation. In the Book of Job, we are told that the Sons of God sang. They were singing because God was the Creator. They didn't really know anything about the love of God then. Now we can sing about our Savior who loves us and who gave Himself for us. What a picture we have here!

"Worthy" reveals that He now fills the entire horizon of praise and worship. Actually, worship is returning to worth, that which belongs to Him: and He is the only One worthy of praise.

"And hast redeemed us to God by thy blood." Changing the pronoun from *"us"* to *"them"* is important. They are praising the Lamb for those yet to be saved on the earth. – The tribulation saints.

"A Kingdom and priests" refers to the tribulation saints. The church will not reign on the earth, but over the earth.

Myriads of Angels Join the Song

And I beheld, and I heard the voice of many angels round about the throne and the beasts and the elders: and the number of them was ten thousand times ten thousand, and thousands of thousands; Saying with a loud voice, Worthy is the Lamb that was slain to receive power and riches, and wisdom, and strength, and honour, and glory, and blessing [Rev. 5:11-12].

When John says, *"Ten thousand times ten thousand, and thousands of thousands,"* it means they are innumerable.

Universal Worship of the Savior and Sovereign

And every creature which is in heaven and on the earth, and under the earth and such as are in the sea, and all that are in them, heard I saying, Blessing and honour, and glory, and power, be unto him that sitteth upon the throne and unto the Lamb for ever and ever, And the four beasts said, Amen. And the four and twenty elders fell down and worshipped him that liveth for ever and ever [Rev. 5:13-14].

Every animate creature of God joins in this universal act of worship, both in heaven and earth. The living creatures add their amen to it, and the church falls down in silent adoration and praise.

As we come to the end of this very remarkable scene in heaven, we see that all praise, honor, and worship must go to the Lord Jesus Christ. If you are not in the habit of praising and worshiping Him, why don't you start right now?

Chapter 6

Theme: *Opening Of The First Six Seals*

<u>Opening of the Seven – Sealed Book</u>

And I saw when the Lamb opened one of the seals and I heard, as it were the noise of thunder, one of the four beasts saying, Come and see. And I saw, and behold a white horse: and a crown was given unto him: and he went forth conquering, and to conquer [Rev. 6:1-2].

Christ will break all the seals, ad seriatium, right in order. He is in full charge, and every creature in heaven is moving at this command. So the four horse men are now going to ride forth. He breaks the seal and say, *"Go."* It is restated by John that he *"saw"* and he *"heard."*

Attempts to determine the symbolism of the rider on the white horse have given rise to many differences of opinion. The preponderate interpretation among commentators is that he represents Christ. They use *Psalm 45* and *Revelation 19* is the support of their position. But most of the contemporary Bible expositors of the premillennial school say that the white horse and rider in Antichrist. We'll take the position that this is the Antichrist.

Opening of the First Seal

This is an imitation of Christ. This is one who pretends to be Christ, who comes forth. We are moving today in the direction of a world dictator. Antichrist does not appear as a villain. After all, Satan's angels are angels of light. That is the platform that antichrist will come in on – world unity and peace. There is a great deal of talking about peace. When Antichrist comes to power. He will talk peace and the world will think that it is entering the millennium when it is actually entering the Great Tribulation. The Great Tribulation comes in like a lamb but it goes out like a lion. A promise of peace is the big lie the world is going to believe. This rider could not be Christ, therefore because Christ is the Lamb in the midst of the throne who, as the Lion of the Tribe of Judah, the Root of David, is directing these events from heaven and is giving orders to the four horsemen to ride Christ is clearly identified in *Revelation 19*. While here, the identity is certainly obscure, which suggests that it is not Christ but an imitation of Him.

Opening of the Second Seal Rider on a Red Horse

And when he had opened the second seal, I heard the second beast say, Come and see. And there went out another horse that was red: and power was given to him that sat thereon to take peace from the earth, and that they should kill one another: and there was given unto him a great sword [Rev. 6:3-4].

The first horseman could not be Christ because when He brings peace to this earth, it is going to be permanent. This is a short lived peace. Immediately, after the white horse went forth, here came the red horse of war on the earth. The peace which the rider on the white horse brought to the earth was temporary and counterfeit. The antichrist presents himself as a ruler who brings peace to the world, but he cannot guarantee it. For God says, *"There is no peace saith my God to the wicked"* *(Isa. 57:21)*. And that passage of Scripture certainly has been fulfilled.

Antichrist will be a phony. He won't bring peace because here goes the fiery red horse of war riding throughout the earth again. And this is going to be a real world war.

Opening of the Third Seal Rider on a Black Horse

And when he had opened the third seal, I heard the third beast say, Come and see. And I beheld, and lo a black horse; and he that sat on him had a pair of balances in his hand. And I heard a voice in the midst of the four beasts says, A measure of the wheat for a penny, and three measures of barley for a penny; and see thou hurt not the oil and the wine [Rev. 6:5-6].

John again says, *"I heard"* and *"I saw."* He just wants to make sure that we know that. The color of the black horse indicates mourning (see *Jer. 4:28, Mal. 3:14*) mourning fully in black. And it also speaks of famine in *Lamentations 4:8-9*. We read, *"...the black horse represents the world wide famine that is to come on the earth."* Always after a war, there is a shortage of foodstuff. This which we are talking about in Revelation in the future. The only reason to make an application today is to show this is not unreasonable. It is going to take place.

Opening of the Forth Seal Rider on A Pale Horse

And when he had opened the fourth seal, I heard the voice of the fourth beast say, Come and see. And I looked, and behold a pale horse: and his name that sat on him was Death, and Hell followed with him. And power was given unto them over the fourth part of the earth, to kill with sword, and with hunger, and with death, and with the beasts of the earth [Rev. 6:7-8].

"Death was his name." Death is no more personalized here than is war – although the rider is given the name of death. There is more involved in physical death than meets the eye, for the human being is more than physical and death is more than cessation of physical activity. While death takes the body, hades is the place where the spirit of a lost man goes (see *Luke 16:23 ASV).*

"Death was his name and Hades followed him." The word for Hades is something unfortunately translated by the word hell as in *Luke 16:23* where, speaking of the rich man and Lazarus.

Hell is a very unfortunate translation there; it is this same word hades and actually it does not refer to hell at all. It speaks of physical death – either where the spirit goes or the grave where the body is placed. In other words, while death takes the body, hades is the place where the spirit of the lost man goes.

The Lord Jesus spoke of it in that way. Sin and death entered the world at the same time. Death is the result of sin. Death evidently has an all-inclusive threefold meaning that we do not ordinarily attach to it. We think of death as referring only to the body:

1. This is physical death, and it refers only to the body. It comes to a man because of Adam's sin.
2. Then there is what is known as spiritual death, which is separation from, and rebellion against God.
3. Finally, there is eternal death, which is eternal separation from God. Unless a man is redeemed, this inevitably follows.

He (Adam) died spiritually, and physical death followed and has come into the human family. During the Great Tribulation, death will ride unbridled.

At the Great White Throne judgment, death will be finally destroyed (see *Rev. 20:14*). This is confirmed by Paul who writes, *"The last enemy that shall be destroyed is death." 1 Cor. 15:26.*

The sword, famine, pestilence, and wild beasts will decimate this earth's population by one fourth. The pale horse represents plague and pestilence that will stalk the earth. It also encompasses the possibility or germ warfare. While the greater part of all city's population could be destroyed by an atomic bomb, the bacteria method might easily wipe out the entire population within a week.

We have seen the riding of the four horsemen, and this follows exactly the pattern that the Lord Jesus gave while He was on the earth. In *Matthew 24:5-8,* in the Olivet Discourse. All these are the beginning of sorrows. This is the opening of the Great Tribulation.

Opening of the Fifth Seal- Prayer of the Martyred Remnant

And when he had opened the fifth seal, I saw under the altar the souls of them that were slain for the word of God, and for the testimony which they held: And they cried with a loud voice saying, How long, O Lord, holy and true, dost thou not judge and avenge our blood on them that dwell on the earth? [Rev. 6:9-10].

This altar is in heaven and is evidently where Christ offered His blood for the sins of the world. The souls mentioned here are the Old Testament Saints. Included with these are those who will be slain in the Great Tribulation Period, as we have already found that one fourth of the population will be wiped out. They are resting on solid Old Testament ground as they plead for justice on the basis of God's Holy Law.

And white robes were given unto every one of them; and it was said unto them, that they should rest yet for a little season, until their fellow-servants also and their brethren, that should be killed as they were, should be fulfilled [Re. 6:11].

In other words, the tribulation saints are to be included with the Old Testament saints in the second resurrection.

Opening of the Sixth Seal – The Day of Wrath Has Come

And I beheld when he had opened the sixth seal, and, lo, there was a great earthquake; and the sun became black as sackcloth of hair, and the moon became as blood; And the stars of heaven fell unto the earth, even as a fig tree casteth her untimely figs, when she is shaken of a mighty wind [Rev 6:12-13].

This is evidently the beginning of the last great day of His wrath is before us. The Great Tribulation opens and closes with these upheavals in the natural universe:

1. The beginning of the Tribulation (compare *Joel 2:30—31 with Acts 2:20)* and
2. The end of the Tribulation (see *Joel 3:9-17; Isa. 13:9-13; 34:1-4; Matt. 24:29).*

What a picture we have here! The earthquakes today are not a fulfillment. They merely show that it could happen as God's Word says it will.

And the heaven departed as a scroll when it is rolled together; and every mountain and island were moved out of their places [Rev. 6:14].

This verse is to be taken quite literally. We see the same thing in *Nahum 1:5* and again in Chapter 20, verse 11.

And the kings of the earth, and the great men, and the rich men, and the chief captains, and they mighty men, and every bondman, and every freeman, hid themselves in the dens and in the rocks of the mountains; And said to the mountains and rocks, Fall on us, and hide us from the face of him that sitteth on the throne, and from the wrath of the Lamb: For the great day of his wrath is come; and who shall be able to stand? [Rev. 6:15-17].

Now there are those on the earth who are praying to rocks and to the mountains to fall upon them because they want to be hidden. Hidden from whom? From the wrath of the Lamb.

This is the great day of the wrath of God. *"The wrath of the Lamb"* is a paradoxical phrase. The wrath of God is the Day of the Lord that day this is spoken of all the way through the Old Testament prophets a day that is coming upon the earth and is yet future. It is called here *"the wrath of the Lamb"* – that is a strange statement. The Bible is filled with paradoxes. A paradox is a proposition that is contrary to received opinion: that is, it is which is seemingly contradictory.

Here we have *"the wrath of the Lamb."* The lamb is a familiar figure of Christ. The apostle John calls Him *"the Lamb slain from the foundation of the world" (Rev. 13:8).* In other words, God did not choose the lamb because it possessed characteristics of Christ. Neither did He choose it for the sacrificial aspect. God created such an animal to represent Christ. Christ is the Lamb Slain before the foundation of the world, before any lamb was ever created.

The Lord Jesus Christ has the qualities of a lamb. He was meek – *Matt. 11:28-29;* He was humble. – Christ washed the feet of His disciples.

But what about *"the wrath?"* Wrath is strange and foreign even to the person of God; God loves the good. God hates evil. God is righteous, God is holy, and He hates that which is contrary to Himself.

Look at this world we are in. It already reveals the wrath of God, the judgement of God. Christ rejected Jerusalem, but He had tears in His eyes when He did so. He still controls the forces of nature, and He uses them in judgement. God has declared war against sin.

"Bless are all they that put their trust in Him" (Ps. 2:10-12).

Chapter 7

Theme: *God Seal A Remnant Of Israel And Saves A Redeemed Company Of Gentiles.*

<u>Reason For The Interlude</u>

And after these things I saw four angels standing on the four corners of the earth, holding the four winds of the earth, that the wind should not blow on the earth, nor on the sea, nor on any tree [Rev. 7:1].

"After this" refers to the tremendous judgment of the previous chapter, the riding of the four horsemen. In the riding of the four horsemen, we have been given a bird eye's view of the Great Tribulation Period, an overall picture and now the details are going to be given to us.

"After this I saw four angels standing on the four corners of the earth." *"Holding firmly the four winds of the earth that no wind might blow on the earth, nor on the sea, nor on any tree."* These would be winds of judgement. God uses wind in judgement, and He controls the wind (*Ps. 148:8*).

The winds of judgement are now to be held back. Nothing can move until God accomplishes His purpose. What is His purpose going to be? A great company is going to be saved, and this reveals that this judgment will accomplish a purpose for God. In our lives as believers, when trouble comes to us- it will either draw us to God or drive us from Him.

And I saw another angel ascending from the east, having the seal of the living God: and he cried with a loud voice to the four angels, to whom it was given to hurt the earth and the sea, Saying Hurt not the earth, neither the sea, nor the trees, till we have sealed the servants of our God in their foreheads [Rev. 7:2-3].

"Another angel" means this is a fifth angel. He is apparently of a higher rank than the other four because he gives them orders.

"He cried with a great voice." In the Greek, this is the phone megale. If you turn phone megale around, you can see where we get our English word megaphone. Megale means *"great;"* phone means noise or voice.

This is an indication that frightful and fearful judgement is getting ready to break upon the earth, and it is therefore necessary to secure the servants of God! The Lord Jesus Himself mentioned this in *Matthew 24:21-22.*

Now what is the mark that is put upon their foreheads? (i.e. Seal). We are not told what it is, and it's not important for the church. We are simply told that they are going to be marked. When the antichrist comes to power, unless they have the mark of the Beast, they cannot buy or trade. This mark of God is in contrast to the mark of the Beast. Some kind of spiritual mark that will be in their lives.

We now have this interlude before the seventh seal is opened. This angel is apparently more than a sergeant; he probably a lieutenant colonel or a general.

He says, *"Hold everything! Hold back the winds of judgement, the winds of the Great Tribulation Period, because we have to seal these folks so they can make it through."*

There will be two great companies sealed, one out of the nation Israel and the other out of the Gentiles. The reason for the interlude between the sixth and seventh seals is to make it through the Great Tribulation Period. The Lord Jesus made it very clear that they will make it through.

Remnant of Israel Sealed

And I heard the number of them which were sealed: and there were sealed an hundred and forty and four thousands of all the tribes of the children of Israel [Rev. 7:4].

When God deals with Israel, however, He deals with numbers and He deals with dates. One hundred forty four thousand is the number sealed from the nation Israel, but we will see that out of the earth there will be a multitude of Gentiles saved - too numerous to count. The seal guarantees that they are going to be delivered.

During the Great Tribulation, 144,000 are going to be saved out of every tribe of the children of Israel. This number does not refer to any group in existence today, nor does it refer to the church. It's very clear that God will have a remnant of His people who are going to be saved.

Of the tribe of Juda were sealed twelve thousand. Of the tribe of Reuben were sealed twelve thousand. Of the tribe of Gad were sealed twelve thousand. Of the tribe of Asher were sealed twelve thousand. Of the tribe of Nepthalim were sealed twelve thousand. Of the Manasses were sealed twelve thousand. Of the tribe of Simeon were sealed twelve thousand. Of the tribe of Levi were sealed twelve thousand. Of the tribe of Issachar were sealed twelve thousand. Of the tribe of Zabulon were sealed twelve thousand. Of the tribe of Joseph were sealed twelve thousand. Of the tribe of Benjamin were sealed twelve thousand [Rev. 7:5-8].

Twelve thousand are sealed out of each tribe. The 144, 000 are divided by twelve and one twelfth is in each tribe, so that we know that John is talking about the children of Israel. We can't spiritualize this and attempt to appropriate it either to themselves or to some group other than the children of Israel. The 144,000 are sealed, especially because they are going to witness during this period, and it is going to cost them a great deal. If they were not sealed, they sure wouldn't be able to make it through. God never leaves Himself without a witness upon this earth.

Redeemed Multitude of Gentiles

After this I beheld, and, lo, a great multitude which no man could number, of all nations, and kindreds, and people, and tongues, stood before the throne, and before the Lamb, clothed with white robes, and palms in their hands; And cried with a loud voice, saying, Salvation to our God who sitteth upon the throne and to the Lamb [Rev. 7:9-10].

"After these things I saw." John is seeing as well as hearing these things.
"And behold, a great multitude which no man could number."
"Out of every nation and out of tribes, and people and tongues." These are Gentiles, people from every tribe and nation under the sun. This means that in the Great Tribulation, the gospel of the kingdom will be preached throughout the world.
"Standing before the throne and before the Lamb."

Here is a great company who have come out of the Great Tribulation Period and are rejoicing in its salvation. They are redeemed and have made it through the Great Tribulation Period.

"The white robes" set before us the righteousness of Christ is which they are clothed.

"Palm branches" is literally in the Greek *"palm trees."* They are a sign of victory, victory in Christ. This is a wonderful, glorious picture that is given to us.

And all the angels stood round about the throne, and about the elders and the four beasts, and fell before the throne on the faces, and worshipped God, Saying, Amen: Blessings, and glory, and wisdom, and thanksgiving, and honour, and power, and might, be unto our God for ever and ever. Amen [Rev. 7:11-12].

This is a fabulous, fantastic scene of universal worship of God by His creatures. The church is here, the Old Testament saints are here, and the tribulation saints are here. And now the angles join in on it. But nowhere in Scripture does it say that angels sing. They are saying this here. However, the important thing to note is that the other companies thank God for their redemption, *"Salvation to our God,"* but the angels do not mention it. They praise God for His attributes and goodness, but not for salvation. Why? They are sinless creatures, not redeemed sinners.

And one of the elders answered, saying unto me, What are these which are arrayed in white robes? And whence came they? And I said unto him, Sir thou knowest. And he said to me, These are they which came out of great tribulation, and have washed their robes, and made them white in the blood of the Lamb [Rev. 7:13-14].

This is a very enlightening passage of Scripture. One of the elders went over to John and said, *"John, who are these believers have arranged in the white robes?"* And John said, *"My Lord, thou knowest."* You know that I don't know. You tell me because I don't know. This is what John is saying here.

And he said to me, *"These are they which came out of great tribulation."*

In the Great Tribulation, we come to a period when there are but two groups: Jews and Gentiles. Where is the church of God? It went to be with Him. The Lord Jesus said *(John 14:2-3).*

The church is with Him in heaven as we move through the Revelation. God today is calling out of the two divisions both Jews and Gentiles, a people for His name that are different – the church- and that church will be taken out of the world.

John makes it clear that this group he sees in the heavens is different from the church. They came through the Great Tribulation. They are identified as redeemed Gentiles who have come out of the Great Tribulation.

Their robes were white, which speaks of the righteousness of Christ. How did they get that righteousness? It is because Christ shed His blood.

The only reason that you and I will be able to stand before God is because Christ paid the penalty for our sins. And it has always been true that God has only one way of saving mankind, and it is by faith in the death and resurrection of Jesus Christ. The gospel is not God asking you to do something; it is God telling you that He has done something for you. The gospel is not your giving something to God; the gospel is God giving something to you. The gift of God is eternal life in Christ Jesus. The gospel is what God has done for us. It's His gift.

Therefore are they before the throne of God, and serve him day and night in his temple: and he that sitteth on the throne shall dwell among them. They shall hunger no more, neither thirst any more; neither shall the sun light on them, nor any heat. For the Lamb, which is in the midst of the throne shall feed them, and shall lead them unto living fountains of waters: and God shall wipe away all tears from their eyes [Rev. 7:15-17].

"Therefore are they before the throne of God, and serve him day and night in his temple," Now we know for sure that this is not the church, for the church is never identified with the temple.

"And He that sitteth on the throne shall spread His tabernacle (tent) over them." This is for their protection. They made it through the Great Tribulation because of the blood of the Lamb. This company of Gentiles are some of the other sheep who will be redeemed but are not a part of the church.

Chapter 8

Theme: *Opening The Seventh Seal*

Opening of the Seventh Seal- Introduction of Seven Trumpets

And when he had opened the seventh seal, there was silence in heaven about the space of half an hour [Rev. 8:1].

"There was silence in heaven about the space of half an hour." The Lord Jesus Christ is still in command. He opens the seven seal, and there is introduced a fanfare of seven trumpets. He directs the action now from heaven. We need to keep that before us through the entire book. Do not lose sight of the fact that revelation presents Him in His glory as the Judge of all the earth.

Now men are not lost because they are sinners. They are lost because they have rejected Jesus, who died for them. If you go into a lost eternity and not accept Christ. He died for you and you simply made His sacrifice for you of no avail. Now this is a very solemn scene. The Lord Jesus Christ orders a halt on all fronts: heaven, hell, and earth. Nothing can move without His permission.

Now, for a belief moment, there is a lull in judgement activity. There is a heavenly hush. The lull before the storm (the calm).

Why is there this strange silence? God's patience is not exhausted. When the sixth seal was opened and nature responded with a mighty convulsion, brave men weakened for a moment. Christ gave them the opportunity to repent. But like the Pharaoh of old who when the heat was taken off. Let this willful heart return to its original intention. Many men will go back to their blasphemous conduct when there is a calm.

"The steps of God from mercy to judgement are always slow, reluctant, and measured." God is reluctant to judge, for His is slow to anger. Judgment is His strange work *(Isa. 28:21)*. Isaiah writes: What is strange about God? That He judges, that He is a God of love, judging His creatures. This silence marks the transition from grace to judgement. God is waiting. He is waiting for you to come to Him. You can come to Him for He is a gracious Savior.

Blowing of the Seven Trumpets

And I saw the seven angels which stood before God; and to them were given seven trumpets [Rev. 8:2].

These *"seven angels"* are introduced to us as a special group. Judgement is getting ready to come upon the earth. This is the lull before the storm of judgment. Before the storm hit, there was a certain stillness.

"Seven trumpets" have a special meaning for Israel. Here is where it is essential to have a knowledge of the Old Testament. In the Book of Numbers, Moses was given instruction by God to make two silver trumpets. Two was the number of witnesses.

These two trumpets were used on the wilderness march (See *Num. 10:2*). When Israel entered the land, the trumpets were used for two other purposes:

1. War
2. Gladness and your solemn days (*Num. 10:9-10*).

A single trumpet is that which we believe corresponds to *"the last trumpet,"* which Paul mentions in *1 Corinthians 15 (1 Cor. 15:51-52)*. Unfortunately, there are some who assume that *"the last trumpet"* of 1 Corinthians 15 is the seventh trumpet of Revelation – there is no relation at all.

"The trump of God" is still His voice – His voice will sound like a trumpet. This is a book of triumph and of victory from our God.

An another angel came and stood at the altar, having a golden censer; and there was given unto him much incense that he should offer it with the prayers of all saints on top the golden altar which was before the throne [Rev. 8:3].

"Another angel" is positively not Christ. The Lord Jesus Christ is no longer in the position of intercessor for the church. We saw in chapters 4-5 that He moved away from that position and was given the seven-sealed book. He is in charge of everything that happens from there on in Revelation. And He is not the intercessor. He is now in the place of judgment. He holds the book of the seven seals, and He directs all the activities from the throne.

The *"golden altar"* is the place where prayer is offered. Christ is not in the place of intercession before the golden altar. He is now upon the throne. Incense is likened to prayer and is a type of prayer. David in *Psalm 141:2*, *"Let my prayer be set forth before thee as incense."*

Incense speaks of the value of Christ's name and works in prayer. The prayers of saints which were offered under the fifth seal (see *Rev. 6:9-11)* were now being answered because of the person and sacrifice of Christ.

And the smoke of the incense, which came with the prayers of the saints, ascended up before God out of the angel's hand [Rev. 8:4].

Prayer is going to be answered because of Christ.

And the angel took the censer, and filled it with the fire of the altar, and cast it into the earth: and there were voices and thundering, and lightnings, and an earthquake [Rev. 8:5].

The high priest of Israel took a censer with him as he carried the blood into the Holy of Holies. Here the ritual is reversed because out of heaven, the censer is hurled upon the earth. In other words, the prayers ascended as incense, and now we have the answer coming down. The tribulation saints had prayed, "Oh God, avenge us! The people of the earth have rejected the death of Christ for the judgement of their sins. Must now bear the judgment for their own sins. The Great Tribulation is going to get under way.

"Thunders" denotes the approach of the coming storm of God's judgement. *"Voices"* reveal that this is the intelligent direction of God and not the purposeless working of natural forces. God is in charge.

"Lightings" follow the thunder. The *"earthquake"* is the earth's response to the severe pressure which will be placed upon it during the judgement of the Great Tribulation Period.

And the seven angels which had the seven trumpets prepared themselves to sound [Rev. 8:6].

Now this is a solemn moment. The half hour silence is over. The prayers of the saints have been heard. The order is issued to prepare to blow. The angels come to attention, and at the blowing of the trumpets, divine wrath is visited upon rebellious men. The blowing of the trumpets does not introduce symbols or secrets. The plagues here are literal plagues. This method today of evaporating the meaning of Scripture by calling it symbolic is just as bad as denying the inspiration of the Word of God. In other words, it is saying that God doesn't mean what He says and that He means something else altogether.

First Trumpet – Trees Burn

The first angel sounded, and there followed hail and fire mingled with blood, and they were cast upon the earth: and the third part of trees was burnt up, and all green grass burnt up [Rev. 8:7].

This is a direct judgment from God. Judgment falls upon plant life, from the grass to the great trees. Every form of botanical life is affected first. Notice, however, that it is only one-third, but it makes a tremendous impact on the earth. Fire, the great enemy, is the instrument God uses. The flood was used in the first global judgment. Now it's going to be fire.

This earth is to be purified by fire. One third of the earth denotes the wide extent of the damage. *"One-third"* means not one fourth or one half: it means one third. Plant life was the first to be created, and it was the first to be destroyed. In the record given in *Genesis 1:11*. God began with the creation of plant life after the order had been brought into the physical globe. This is a literal judgement upon plant life in the same way that the seventh plague of Egypt was literal (See *Exod. 9:18-26*).

Now there is a striking similarity between the plagues in Egypt and the trumpet judgments – this is no accident.

When hail came down on Egypt, we are told that *"...the hail smote every herb of the field, and brake every tree of the field."*

Exod. 9:25- it was 100 percent destruction in Egypt: it will be one third of the earth.

Second Trumpets -Seas Become Blood

And the second angel sounded, and as it were a great mountain burning with fire was cast into the sea: and the third part of the sea became blood; And the third part of the creatures which were in the sea, and had life, died; and the third part of the ships were destroyed [Rev. 8:8-9].

The sea, which occupies most of the earth's surface, is next affected by this direct judgment of God. The separation of the land and the sea occurred on the same day in which plant life appeared (see *Gen. 1:9-10).*

Note: John does not say that a burning mountain was cast into the sea, but rather he indicates that a great mass or force *"as it were a great mountain burning with fire as [thrown] cast into the sea"* – as it were a great mountain.

The mountain represents something as literal and tangible as that which we have in *Jeremiah 51:25,* where the Lord is talking about Babylon:

This literal mass falls into the literal sea, one-third becomes literal blood, and one-third of all the literal living and creatures in the literal sea die a literal death. Nothing can be plainer than that. Also, one third of the literal ships of all literal nations are literal destroyed. Now there is no use in trying to find some symbol. John doesn't say that this is symbolic.

Third Trumpet – Fresh Waters Become Bitter

And the third angel sounded, and there fell a great star from heaven, burning as it were a lamp, and it fell upon the third part of the rivers, and upon the fountains of water; And the name of the star is Wormwood: and the third part of the waters became wormwood; and many men died of the water, because they were bitter [Rev. 8:10-11].

Now we are living in a world today where a great deal is being said about pollution and it is real problem. Self-preservation is considered to be the first law of nature, and man wants to hang on to this little earth: In the Great Tribulation, the flesh water is polluted and the drinking water for mankind is contaminated, that is one-third of it is. Here is Revelation, the sweet waters are made bitter by a meteor, a star out of heaven. The tree that Moses put into the water speak of the cross of Christ.

"Wormwood" is a name used metaphonically in the Old Testament.
1. Idolatry of Israel
2. Calamity and sorrow
3. False judgment

This star is literal and is a meteor containing a poison that contaminates one-third of the earth's flesh water supply. The star's name suggests that this is a judgment upon man for idolatry and injustice. Calamity and sorrow are the natural compensation from man because of the judgement.

Fourth Trumpet – Sun, Moon, And Stars Smitten

And the fourth angel sounded, and the third part of the sun was smitten, and the third part of the moon, and the third part of the stars; so as the third part of them was darkened, and the day shone not for a third part of it, and the night likewise [Rev. 8:12].

Another phase of creation upon which mankind on the earth is solely dependent for light life is the sun. To a lesser degree, man is dependent on the moon and stars. It was on the fourth day of recreation that these heavenly bodies appeared. The laws of nature are radically altered by these disturbances.

And I beheld, and heard an angel flying through the midst of heaven, saying with a loud voice, Woe, woe, woe, to the inhabiters of the earth by reason of the voices of the trumpet of three angels, which are yet to sound! [Rev. 8:13].

When the fourth trumpet is blown, the announcement is made of a peculiar intensity of woe and judgement that is coming on the earth. The last three trumpets are separated from the other four: they are *"woe"* trumpets.

Chapter 9

Theme: *The fifth and sixth trumpets*

Fifth Trumpet- Fallen Star And Plague Of Locusts

And the fifth angel sounded, and I saw a star fall from heaven unto the earth: and to him was given the key to the bottomless pit [Rev. 9:1].

Here in verse 1, we describe the scene as the fifth angel sounds like a trumpet and a star falls from heaven. Notice the proper meaning of the "bottomless pit" is the long shaft (or pit or well) of the abyss.

"I saw a star fall from heaven unto the earth." We have already seen two stars and said they were literal stars, or meteors, that fell to the earth. Meteors are the shooting stars. But here we have a different kind of star because it is called *"him"* and acts with intelligence. We are talking now about an unusual person. This star is different. Therefore, from the stars mentioned at the sounding of the fourth trumpet. This star not only acts with intelligence, but he is given a key that he uses – no inanimate star could do this.

We believe that this star is Satan. Now the reason for interpreting this star as Satan is abundant. The prophet Isaiah writes *Isa. 14:12; Luke 10:18*. Also,

Paul writes *2 Cor. 11:14.* Satan transformed himself into an angel of light. These scriptures confirm the position that Satan is in view here. John well states later that Satan was put out of heaven and cast to the earth (see *Rev. 12:7-9).* Now, if we established the fact that the "star" is Satan being cast out of heaven, then what does he do?

He goes down and takes the key to the abyss, which apparently means that God is permitting him to do so. A key denotes authority and power, and this is given to him by God. It is the permissive will of God.

"The long shaft of the abyss" means the long shaft leading to the abyss. The abyss is the bottomless pit which will be seen in chapter 20, verse 3. The abyss and hades may be synonymous terms, but the abyss and hell are not the same. The abyss is a very literal place. The Lord now holds the key to the abyss (See *Rev. 1:18).* The idea that heaven and hell are mythological and heaven is a beautiful isle somewhere is not the teaching of the Word of God. The teaching of the Word of God is that heaven is as literal as the place where you live today and that hell is equally as real as the place where you now live.

During the last part of the Great Tribulation, the key to the abyss is given to Satan, and he is given a freedom that he has never had before. This explains why men cannot die during this period. Satan wants to keep them alive: he does not want his army decimated at all.

And he opened the bottomless pit; and there arose a smoke out of the pit, as the smoke of a great furnace; and the sun and the air were darkened by reason of the smoke of the pit [Rev. 9.2].

Out of the shaft, like a great erupting volcano, smoke will cover the entire earth. This smog of the most vicious type. The literal interpretation of this verse is the correct and most satisfying one.

And there came out the smoke locust upon the earth: and unto them was given power, as the scorpions of the earth have power. And it was commanded them that they should not hurt the grass of the earth, neither any green things, neither any tree; but only those men, which have not the seal of God in their forehead [Rev.9:3-4].

Now this beggar description, John uses symbolic language which describes creatures so frightful that this is the only way he could speak of them. These locusts are of a very unusual character. As Govett remarks (*The Apocalypse Expounded by Scripture pp. 185-186)*, they are ***"no common locusts,"*** and he gives the following reasons:

1. For they eat no vegetable productions
2. The locust of the earth have no King (*Prov. 30:27);* these have:
3. In the plague of Egypt the inspired recorder had said, *"Before them there were no such locust as they, neither after them shall be such"* (*Exod. 10:14)*.
4. Yet they are literal creatures resembling the literal animals named: the lion, the horse, the scorpion, the man.

This is a plague of locusts which is as literal as the plague of locusts in Egypt. Joel prophesied of a coming plague of locust *(Joel 1)!* Again, a working knowledge of the Old Testament is essential to the understanding of Revelation. The difference between the locusts here and locusts in Joel is the character of the locust and the object of the destruction. They sting as scorpions, and their objects are evil men.

And to them it was given that they should not kill them, but that they should be tormented five months: and their torment was as the torment of a scorpion, when he striketh a man [Rev. 9:5].

The scorpion is shaped like a lobster and lives in damp places. His sting is in his tail: though it is not fatal, it is very painful indeed. This is the picture we are given here. Therefore we can see that believers living during the Great Tribulation who will be acquainted with the Old Testament will understand what John is talking about regarding these scorpions.

And in those days shall men seek death, and shall not find it; and shall desire to die, and death shall flee from them [Rev. 9:6].

Satan is given the key to this long shaft which evidently is what is called Sheol in the Old Testament and hell; hades in the New Testament, the shaft leads to the abyss where the spirit of the dead of the ages past have gone.

Satan does not want his crowd to die and it is only his crowd that are attacked by these locusts. Men during this period try to commit suicide and are unable to do it – this reveals something of the awfulness of that day. Satan wants them here because a battle between light and darkness is being waged.

And the shapes of the locust were like unto horses prepared unto battle; and on their heads were as it were crowns like gold, and their faces were as the faces of men. And they had hair as the hair of women, and their teeth were as the teeth of lions. And they had breastplates, as it were breastplates of iron; and the sound of their wings was as the sound of chariots of many horses running to battle. And they had tails like unto scorpions, and there were stings in their tails and their power was to hurt men five months [Rev. 9:7-10].

We can agree that this is a frightful and unnatural description. A little closer examination, however, will reveal a stalking similarity to the locust of Palestine. The faces of locusts resemble the faces of men. And the antennae of the locust are compared to a girl's hair. Joel compares the teeth of the locust with those of a lion (see *Joel 1:6)*. But there are those today who have attempted to liken this description of the locust to the airplane. Now "Their power was to hurt men five months." It will be five months of unspeakable agony for those who have been attacked by these unnatural locusts.

And they had a king over them, which is the angel of the bottomless pit. Whose name in the Hebrew tongue is Abaddon but in the Greek tongue hath his name Apollyon [Rev. 9:11].

These locusts are further differentiated from ordinary locusts because they have a King over them. *Proverbs 30:27* says of natural locusts that they have no King! The king or leader of these locusts is probably one of the fallen angels, the chief hence – man of Satan, and he is permitted to lead an invasion of the earth for the first time. This is something that's rather frightening. His name in Hebrew means *"Destruction"* and in the Greek, it means *"the destroyer."*

One woe is past; and, behold, there come two woes more hereafter [Rev. 9:12].

Now the first woe was introduced to us in the last half of the Great Tribulation Period and it had a duration of five months. Apparently, the last two woes will cover the remainder of that period. The warning here indicates that worse things are to follow, and the next trumpet reveals that this was not just an idle warning.

Sixth Trumpet – Angels Loosed At River Euphrates

And the sixth angel sounded, and I heard a voice from the four horns of the golden altar which is before God, Saying to the sixth angel, which had the trumpet. Loose the four angels which are bound in the great river Euphrates [Rev. 9:13-14].

When the sixth angel blew the trumpet a command came from the horns of the golden altar. That golden altar speaks of prayer; that is what it spoke of in the tabernacle here on earth.

This is where the angel offered prayer at the beginning of the blowing of the trumpet (see *Rev. 8:3*). The sixth angel not only blows the trumpet, but is also given a command to loose the four angels bound at the river Euphrates. This angel receivers in turn, his orders from a voice that was there at the horns of the golden altar. It is a voice of Christ. He has now ripped off the seventh seal, which led into the trumpets and which will lead into the seven personalities and the seven bowls of wrath. The angels who are bound are evidently evil. Why would they be bound if they were not evil? Why were they bound at this particular location at the Euphrates River? Through hard to explain the prominence of this area in Scripture can not be overlooked.

The Garden of Eden was somewhere in this section. The sin of men began here. The first murder was committed here. The first war was fought here. Here was where the flood began and spread over the earth. Here is where the Tower of Babel was erected. To this area were brought the Israelites of the Babylonian captivity. Babylon was the foundation of idolatry. Here's the final surge of sin on the earth during the Great Tribulation.

Now the Euphrates actually marks the division between East and West. Zechariah locates Babylon as the last stand of false religion (see *Zech. 5*). This is where Satan's last stand will take place.

And the four angels were loosed, which were prepared for an hour, and a day, and a month, and a year, for to slay the third part of men. And the number of the army of the horsemen were two hundred thousand thousand: and I heard the number of them [Rev. 9:15-16].

And the four angels were loosed, who had been prepared for the hour, day, month, and year. You will have to take that literally because we don't know how else we would take it. The very hour is marked out.

"That they might kill the third of men." At the blowing of the sixth trumpet, one third of the population of mankind will be removed. Now we have already seen a fourth removed, and now a third is removed. Over one half of the population of the earth will be destroyed in the Great Tribulation Period. No wonder the Lord said, *"And except those days should be short-hand, there should no flesh be saved..." (Matt. 24:22).*

The size of the army is stupendous. It's numbered at 200 million. Now the great population is in the East today. What is spoken of here in this passage is the wholesale invasion of the earth by the demon world represented in the locusts.

And thus I saw the horse in the vision, and them that sat on them, having breastplates of fire, and of jacinth, and brimstone: and the heads of the horses were as the heads of lions; and out of their mouths issued fire and smoke and brimstone. By these three was the third part of men killed, by the fire, and by the smoke, and by the brimstone, which issued out of their mouths [Rev. 9:17-18].

The following description of the horse men further confirms this fact. Now notice that the colors are as striking as the horsemen are unnatural. *"Fire"* is fiery red *"hyacinth"* is the same color as the flower-dull, dark blue; *"Brimstone"* is light yellow.

The horse is the animal of war (see *Job 39:19-25).* The underworld is now making war on mankind. These creatures from the underworld are unnatural, demon-controlled. Hellish forces will be at work during this period. These three plagues mentioned here are literal plagues. The fire is literal, the smoke is literal, and the brimstone is literal. The same thing took place at the destruction of Sodom and Gomorrah. Now I believe that during the Great Tribulation Period will actually be worse than that of Sodom and Gomorrah.

At this point, one-third of the population is killed. One third of nature had already been affected but mankind had not been touched with a judgement of this magnitude. Remember that a fourth part had been slain under the fourth seal.

For their power is in their mouth, and in their tails; for their tails were like unto serpents, and had heads, and with them they do hurt [Rev. 9:19].

These unnatural horses can kill with their mouths. The weirdest feat of all is that, instead of horse hair for tails, they have serpents which are also used in destroying mankind.

And the rest of them which were not killed by these plagues yet repented not of the works of their hands, that they should not worship devils, and idols of gold, and silver, and brass, and stone, and of wood: which neither can see, nor hear, nor walk: Neither repented they of the murders, nor of their sorceries, or of their fornication, nor of their thefts [Rev. 9:20-21].

"Sorceries" is the Greek word pharmakeion from which we get our English word pharmacy. Pharmacy means *"drugs."* What were called drugstores back in the day, today are called pharmacies. The Great Tribulation will be a period when the use of drugs will not be controlled. Drugs will play a large part in the lives of the unsaved and serve several purposes. The drug will enable them to bear the judgement of the Great Tribulation.

Drugs will also figure largely in the religion of that day. That will be the religion of that day. There will be a regular drug culture and drug religion in the days of the Great Tribulation. People will resort to everything that will deaden the pain of lifting them out of trouble at that time. Liquor will be very prominent as it is now today.

Drugs are used today in practically every modern cult which uses sex as a drawing card. We are told here that they were guilty not only of sorceries, of indulging in drunkenness and in drugs, but also of fornications that lead to thefts. Sorceries, fornication, and robbery will increase and a greater emphasis will be placed upon them. Antichrist will use three of these to bring mankind into subjection to himself.

Mankind will easily be lured in that day. Under the influence of drugs, he will accept anything. Drugs and liquor will put the antichrist over. Those today who are not standing for the Word of God are easy prey for the cult.

2 Thess. 2:11-12: Paul writes, *"And for this cause God shall send them strong delusion, that they should believe a lie: That they all might be damned who believed not the truth, but had pleasure in unrighteousness."*

When you reject the gospel and shut your heart to God, you are wide open for the big lie when it comes.

Chapter 10

Theme: *Interlude Between The Sixth And Seventh Trumpets*

The Strong Angel With The Little Book

And I saw another mighty angel. Come down from heaven, clothed with a cloud: and a rainbow was upon this head, and his face was as it were the sun, and his feet as pillars of fire [Rev. 10:1].

"And I saw another strong angel." Another means that it is another of the same kind. The other strong angel to whom we were introduced way back in *Revelation 5:2.* There was no argument there: it was not Christ. Through all angels are the servants of Christ. In this final book, of the Bible, this is evidently the special envoy of Christ, bearing all the credentials of his exalted position. The presence of Christ, the One who is in the midst of the throne.

He is *"clothed with a cloud."* This is his uniform as a special envoy from Christ. The clouds of glory are associated with the second coming of Christ, but the angel described here is not coming in clouds of glory, but he is clothed with a cloud. Furthermore, this is not the second coming of Christ to the earth to establish His Kingdom: rather, this angel announces that He is coming soon.

"And the rainbow was upon his head." This is the cap for his uniform and is a reminder of God's covenant with man. This rainbow indicates that God will not send a flood to destroy man again.

"And his face was as the sun.:"This is his badge of identification. This is the signature of the glorified Christ (*Rev. 1: 16*). It does not follow that this one must therefore be the Son of God. Moses' face shone after he had been in the presence of God (see *Exod.34:29*).

This angel's face is shining because he has come out from the presence of Christ. This angel here is not Christ, but he is what it says: an angel, another great mighty angel.

"And his feet as pillars of fire." This is still part of his uniform. He has come to make a special and solemn announcement of coming judgment. All of these features by identification are his credentials and connect him to the person of Christ as His special envoy. The Lord Jesus is running everything at this particular point. He is the Judge of all the earth.

And he had in his hand a little book open: and he set his right foot upon the sea, and his left foot on the earth, And cried with a loud voice, as when a lion roareth: and when he had cried, seven thunders uttered their voices [Rev. 10:2-3].

Now there are several reasons that this little book or scroll is the seven-sealed book that we have seen before. One reason is simply because it is the only book that has been before us. And it is not identified in any other way than it is called *"a little book."* This little book, if it is the same as the seven-sealed book, was originally in the hands of the Father in heaven (see *Rev. 5:1*). It should be noted now it is first transferred to the nail-pierced hands of God the Son. It was given to the Lord Jesus, who was the Only One who could open it.

After He removes the seas, the Lord Jesus Christ transfers the book to the angel, who finally gives it to John to eat. This is the book of the title deed of the earth and it contains the judgment of the Great Tribulation by which the Lord Jesus is coming to power. The book is now open and the judgements are on display. This book is the angel's authority for claiming both the sea and the earth for Christ. He puts one foot on the sea and the other foot upon the earth, and he is claiming both for God.

The earth is His and the fullness thereof (see *Ps. 24:1).* This angel now claims the earth and the sea for the Lord Jesus Christ. Now the Kingdoms of this world will become the Kingdoms of the Lord Jesus Christ through judgment. As Creator and Redeemer, the world belongs to Him. The book is described here as *"a little book"* because the time of the Great Tribulation is not going to be long. We have come here to sort of the half way mark, and we are going to be told that there is not much more time left.

The Great Tribulation is really a short time. The Lord Jesus said it was a brief time. Daniel labeled it as seven years, which certainly is not long. The *"seven thunders"* is God's amen to the angel's claim. *Psalms 29:3;* and in *Job 37:5.* The seven thunders here are the voice of God.

And when the seven thunders had uttered their voices, I was about to write: and I heard a voice from heaven saying unto me, Seal up those things which the seven thunders uttered, and write them not [Rev. 10:4].

The seven thunders therefore were intelligible. This confirmation was also a statement. John was a scribe, and he was taking down the visions as they were given to him (See *Rev 1:11).* He was about to write what the seven thunders had spoken, he heard it, and they were audible words- but he was forbidden to do so. Although Jesus Christ is being revealed in this Book, there are a great many things that God is not telling us.

And the angel which I saw stand upon the sea and upon the earth lifted up his hand to heaven, and sware by him that liveth for ever and ever, who created heaven, and the things that therein are, and the earth, and the things that therein are, and the sea, and the things which are therein that there should be time no longer [Rev. 10:5-6].

Now, this angel makes it clear that he could not be Christ, since he takes an oath by the eternal Creator. He *"lifted up his right hand to heaven, and sware"* – he took an oath by the eternal Creator – *"by Him that liveth for ever and ever."* If they were Christ, he would swear by himself *(Heb. 6:13)*; the writer to the Hebrew says.

The angel swore by another, not by himself because he is not God and therefore he is not the Lord Jesus. The Lord Jesus Christ is the eternal God. The angel is telling the elect that it is not going to be long. He is saying to them. *"Don't worry He that endures to the end, the same shall be saved."* Why? Because they are sealed and they are going to make it through the Great Tribulation Period.

This is likewise in answer to the prayer of the martyrs in *Revelation 6:10*. And also it is the fulfillment of what we call the Lord's Prayer, *"Thy Kingdom come"* (see *Matt. 6:10).*

But in the days of the voice of the seventh angel, when he shall begin to sound, the mystery of God should be finished, as he hath declared to his servants the prophets [Rev. 10:7].

This all occurs when the seventh angel prepares to blow the trumpet. This would indicate that the seventh trumpet brings us to the conclusion of the Great Tribulation. At this time, the mystery of God is finally made clear.

John Eats The Little Book

And the voice which I heard from heaven spake unto me again, and said, Go and take the little book which is open in the hand of the angel which standeth upon the sea and upon the earth [Rev. 10:8].

Now, this order comes from Christ in heaven as He is directing every operation recorded in the Book of Revelation. He is in full charge. Revelation is the book that glorifies our wonderful Saviour. He is the Judge of all the earth here, and we see Him as God has highly exalted Him and given Him a name above every name. John has apparently returned to the earth in Spirit because the little book which was formerly in the hand of God the Father is now transferred to John.

And I went unto the angel, and said unto him, Give me the little book. And he said unto me, Take it, and eat it up; and it shall make thy belly bitter, but it shall be in thy mouth sweet as honey. And I took the little book out of the angel's hand, and ate it up; and it was in my mouth sweet as honey: and as soon as I had eaten it, my belly was bitter [Rev. 10:9-10].

John becomes a participant in the great drama which is unfolding before us. He is required to do a very strange thing, one that has a very typical meaning. He eats the little book at the instructions of the angel and the results are bittersweet. Eating the little book means to receive the Word of God with faith. This is the teaching of the Word of God, for in *Jeremiah 15:16*, we read: Jeremiah likens the appropriation of the Word to eating it.

Ezekiel does the same thing (*Ezek. 3:1-3*). The role here is not a bread roll, but the scroll of that day. Ezekiel said that he ate it and it was just like cake. That's what the Word of God is to the believers.

The part of the Word of God taken by John was judgement. It was sweet because the future is sweet. John eagerly received the Word of God but when he saw that more judgement was to follow it brought travail of soul and sorrow of heart. It was sweet in his mouth and bitter in his digestive system.

And he said unto me, Thou must prophesy again before many peoples, and nations, and tongues, and kings [Rev. 10:11].

You can be sure of one thing, that John was properly integrated. He believed that all nations, all people, all tongues, and all colors ought to hear the Word of God. They need to hear it because they need to be warned that judgment is coming. If they go through the Great Tribulation, they will soon recognize that it is not the millennium – in fact, they will feel as if they have entered hell itself. We are not quite halfway through the Book of Revelation.

This new series of prophecies will begin chapter 12, and it will reveal the fact that there was a great deal more to say. Now the study of prophecy will have a definite effect on your life. It will either bring you closer to Christ or take you farther from Christ.

Chapter 11

Theme: *Interlude Between Sixth And Seventh Trumpets; The Seventh Trumpet Blown*

Date for the Ending of "The Time of The Gentles"

And there was given me a reed like unto a rod: and the angel stood, saying, Rise, and measure the temple of God, and the altar, and them that worship therein. But the court which is without the temple leave out, and measure it not; for it is given unto the Gentiles: and the holy city shall thy tread under foot forty and two months [Rev. 11:1-2].

Here we deal with an indication of projected periods for the close of the Great Tribulation. We are dealing with that period that the Lord Jesus spoke of in *Luke 21:24. "...and Jerusalem shall be trodden down of the Gentiles until the times of the Gentiles be fulfilled."* Jerusalem is still trodden down by the Gentiles. When we come to the last half of the Great Tribulation Period, the time of the Gentiles will run out half way: Forty-two months.

"And there was given me a reed like a rod." Every time you see the beginning of measurements, in either the Old or New Testament, it indicates that God is beginning to deal with the nation Israel (see Jer. 31:38-39; Zech. 2).

This reed is like a rod: a rod is used by a shepherd. In *Psalm 2:9*, we see that a rod is used for chastisement and judgment. What are we dealing with here is a measurement given for the Time of the Gentiles, after which judgment will come upon them. The rod is also for comfort.

Therefore, we have both judgment and solace in this chapter. *"The temple of God"* is limited to the Holy Place (Notice that *"holy place"* is the literal rendering) and the Holy of Holies. The temple of God places us back on Old Testament ground. There's no temple given to the church. The church is a temple of the Holy Spirit today; that's believers (not a building) are the temple of the Holy Spirit.

"The altar" refers to the golden altar of prayer since the altar for burnt offering was not in the temple proper but in the outer court. Even the worshipers are to be measured. John is told to use and measure not only the Holy Place and the altar but also them that worship therein. God does count the number of those who worship Him.

"And the count which is without the temple cast out [Gn: ekbale, throw out] and measure it not."

"For it is given to the nations [that is the Gentiles] declares that although this period still belongs to the Gentiles, their dominion is limited to forty-two months." As have said this confirms the words of the Lord Jesus in *Luke 21:24*.

"Forty and two months" is the three and one half year period identified with the last half of the Great Tribulation Period. We find this repeated in *Revelation 13:5*. This is the last half of the reign of Antichrist here upon this earth. Here the Great Tribulation is divided into two equal parts. This

"week" of Daniel is seven years, and this seven-year period is the seventieth week of Daniel or the Great Tribulation Period.

Duration of The Prophesying Of The Two Witnesses

And I will give power unto my two witnesses, and they shall prophesy a thousand two hundred and threescore days clothed in sackcloth [Rev. 11:3].

There is a great deal of difference of opinion as to the identity of the two witnesses. They are introduced to us without any suggestion as to who they are. They are human witnesses seems certain from the description given of them. Two is the required number of witnesses according to the Law *(Deut. 17:6)*. The Lord Jesus said the same thing relative to the church *(Matt 18:16)*.

Scripture had always required two witnesses to bear testimony to anything before it was to be heard. Therefore, we can definitely say that these witnesses are human beings. These witnesses are two lampstands. They are lights in the world.

"And they shall prophesy a thousand two hundred and threescore days." The first half seems to fit the text more accurately because they testify until the beast appears and then they are martyred (killed).

"Clothed in sackcloth" is the garb better suited to the period of the Law than of grace. It is becoming both to Elijah and John the Baptist.

These are the two olive trees and the two candlesticks standing before the God of the earth. And if any man will hurt them, fire proceedeth out of their mouth, and devoureth their enemies: and if any man will hurt them, he must in this manner be killed [Rev. 11:4-5].

Everything here is associated with the Old Testament. The two olive trees immediately suggest the vision in Zechariah 4. These lampstands are two individuals: Joshua and Zerubbabel.

These two witnesses are lights before the powers of darkness. These men are accorded miraculous power to bring fire down from heaven. They are filled with the Holy Spirit.

These two witnesses are immortal and immune to all attacks until their mission is completed. All of God's men are immortal until God is through with them is a wonderful, confronting thought for today. And when He is through with you, He will remove you from the earth.

These have the power to shut heaven, that it rain not in the days of their prophecy: and have power over waters to turn them to blood, and to smite the earth with all plagues, as often as they will [Rev. 11:6].

These two witnesses are granted unlimited authority. They control rainfall on the earth and they can turn the water into blood. It certainly reminds us of both Elijah and Moses.

"And to smite the earth" – they are given the same power Christ will have when He returns (See *Rev. 19:15*).

"With every plague" suggest the plagues Moses imposed on Egypt, but the plagues here are greater in number as the territory is more vast.

"As often as they wish" reveals the confidence God places in these faithful servants.

And when they shall have finished their testimony, the beast that ascended out of the bottomless pit shall make war against them, and shall overcome them, and kill them [Rev. 11:7].

The witnesses will finish their testimony. In the midst of the week, the antichrist, who is the beast, the man of sin who is moving to power, will bring back first the Roman Empire. Then, when he gets the whole world under his control, he will not hesitate to overcome and destroy these two witnesses. These witnesses live up to their name. Martus is the Greek word for *"witness;"* we get our English word martyr from that.

And their dead bodies shall lie in the street of the great city, which spiritually is called Sodom and Egypt, where also our Lord was crucified [Rev. 11:8].

These men are not given even a decent burial. This reveals the crude, cold barbarism of the last days, which will be covered with but a thin veneer of culture. The word used for bodies (carcasses) denotes the contempt and hatred the world will have for the two witnesses. They are treated as dead animals.

"The great city" in Jerusalem. It is likened unto Sodom by Isaiah (See *Isa. 1:10).* It is called Egypt because the world has entered into every fiber of it's life. – social and political. It is conclusively identified as Jerusalem by the sad designation, *"where also their Lord was crucified."*

And they of the people and kindreds and tongues and nations shall see their dead bodies three days and a half, and shall not suffer their dead bodies to be put in graves [Rev. 11:9].

After Christ was crucified, even Pilate permitted His friends to take down the body and give it a respectable burial, but not so with the two witnesses.

The world will be startled to hear they are dead. Some will be skeptical. This is the worst indignity that a depraved world could vent upon the men who denounced them and their wicked ways. They will decide to just leave the bodies out there and keep the camera on them. Three and one-half days, they are laying there.

And they that dwell upon the earth shall rejoice over them, and make merry, and shall send gifts one to another because these two prophets tormented them that dwelt on the earth [Rev. 11:10].

The death of the two witnesses is an occasion for the high carnival on the earth. *"And shall send gifts one to another"* indicates a lovely occasion on the surface, but this is the Devil's Christmas. Here is the celebration of what antichrist has done instead of the celebration of the coming of Christ to Bethlehem.

And after three days and an half the Spirit of life from God entered into them, and they stood upon their feet: and great fear fell upon them which saw them [Rev. 11:11].

While the world is celebrating in jubilation, the death of these witness and while television cameras are focused upon them.

The witnesses will stand on their feet. The scriptural word for resurrection is used here – the Greek word histeme – *"They stood upon their feet."* These witnesses are among the tribulation saints who have a part in the first resurrection (See *Rev. 20:4-6).*

And they heard a great voice from heaven saying unto them, come up hither And they ascended up to heaven in a cloud and their enemies beheld them [Rev. 11:12].

Now they are caught up in heaven. We have the resurrection of the two witnesses in verse 11 and the ascension of the two witnesses in verse 12. The cloud of glory is associated with the ascension and coming of Christ also.

Doom of the Second Woe -Great Earthquake

And the same hour was there a great earthquake, and the tenth part of the city fell, and in the earthquake were slain of men seven thousand: and the remnant were affrighted, and gave glory to the God of heaven [Rev. 11:13].

Now this number of the slain was to be added to those already slain. A fourth of the population of the world was slain at first, and then a third of the population of the world.- totaling over one half- and now seven thousand more are killed. The earthquake seems to be limited to the city of Jerusalem, just as it was when Christ rose from the dead (see **Matt. 28:2**) and also at His crucifixion (see *Matt. 27:51-52).*

Seven thousand names of men were killed in the earthquake. An idiom to indicate they were men of prominence who went alone with Antichrist, who made headlines when Antichrist came to power.

The second woe is past; and, behold, the third woe cometh quickly [Rev. 11:14].

And the seventh angel sounded; and there were great voices in heaven, saying, The kingdoms of this world are become the kingdom of our Lord, and of his Christ; and he shall reign for ever and ever. And the four and twenty elders, which sat before God on the seats, fell upon their faces, and worshipped God, Saying We give thee thanks, O Lord God Almighty, which art, and wast, and art to come; because thou hast taken to thee thy great power, and hast reigned. And the nations were angry, and thy wrath is come and the time of the dead, that they should be judged, and that thou shouldest give reward unto they servants the prophets, and to the saints, and them that fear thy name, small and great; and shouldest destroy them which destroy the earth [Rev. 11:15-18].

In the middle of all the woes and judgements of the Great Tribulation Period, this is inserted for the encouragement of the believers who will be left on the earth, those who were sealed. The blowing of the seventh trumpet is of the utmost significance and is a special relevance in understanding the remainder of this book. The program of God bridges us chronologically to the breathtaking entrance of eternity, where the mystery of God is finally unraveled.

This section is a summary, a syllabus, or a capsule synopsis of events up to the door of eternity. The following list will help focus these events in our minds:

1. *"Great voices in heaven"* follow the blowing of the seventh trumpet. There was silence in heaven at the opening of the seventh trumpet and the seventh seal. God's created intelligence: can see the end now and is jubilant in anticipation of the termination of evil being so close at hand.

2. *"The kingdom of the world (cosmos is become (the kingdom) or our Lord and of His Christ, and He shall reign unto the ages of the ages (for ever and ever)."* It is not kingdom (plural) but kingdom (singular), which denotes the fact that the kingdoms of this world are at present under Satan, to whom there is no distinction of nations. Actually, all of the kingdoms of this world are Satan's. It is going to become the kingdom *"of our Lord, and of His Christ."* It is going to be delivered to the Lord Jesus Christ, and He is going to rule. The Lord Jesus is coming to put down the rebellion. The seventh trumpet is moving along step by step, toward eternity.

3. *"And the twenty-four elders, sitting before God on their thrones, fell upon their faces, and worshipped God, saying We give thanks to you, O Lord God the Almighty, who art and who wast; because thou hast taken thy great power and didst reign."* This will be the answer to our prayer, *"They Kingdom came. Thy will be done in earth, as it is in heaven"* (*Matt. 6:10*).

4. *"The nations were angry (wrath)"* reveals the fact that the stubborn rebellion of man will continue right down to the very end. The stubborn heart of man is in rebellion against God. This old nature, this carnal nature that you and I have, is not obedient to God. That's exactly what Paul says *(Rom. 8:7)*. The human family could not bring this Old nature under control: that is the reason God is going to get rid of it someday.

5. The nations were angry because *"thy wrath came."* Man is getting worse and worse.

6. *"And the time (period) of the dead to be judged"* brings us to the Great White Throne judgement of the lost dead (see *Rev. 20:11-15*).

7. *"And to give the reward to your servants, the prophets, the saints, and to them that fear thy name, the small and great."*

8. *"And to destroy those who destroy (corrupt, the destroyers as well as Satan."* Peter warns us of Satan (*1 Pet. 5:8*).

And the temple of God was opened in heaven, and there was seen in his temple the ark of his testament: and there were lightnings, and voices, and thunderings, and earthquake, and great hail {Rev. 11:19].

When we see the church again, it will be in the New Jerusalem, and we are told definitely that there is no temple there. Here there is a temple in heaven. The temple which Moses made was made after the pattern in heaven.

"And the sanctuary (temple) of God in heaven was opened" means that *God is dealing now with Israel."*

"Was opened" indicates worship and access to God. All of this point to the nation Israel for the church has no temple.

"And the ark of His covenant was seen in His sanctuary (temple)" reminds us that we are dealing with a covenant- making and covenant keeping God. Lightnings and voices and thunders and an earthquake and great hail "speak of judgement yet to come."

Chapter 12

Theme: *Seven Performers During The Great Tribulation*

The Woman- Israel

And there appeared a great wonder in heaven; a woman clothed with the sun, and the moon under her feet, and upon her head a crown of twelve stars: And she being with child cried, travailing in birth, and pained to delivered [Rev. 12:1-2].

The important thing here is: "Who is the woman?" The theme of this chapter is the final conflict between Israel and Satan. Now the identifying marks of the woman are the sun, moon, and stars. These belong to Israel as seen in Joseph's dream (see *Gen. 37:9-10).*

Old Jacob interpreted the sun, moon, and stars to mean himself, Rachel and Joseph's brothers. And they did bow down before Joseph before things were over with (although Rachel had died by that time).

Now the woman is a sign in heaven, although her career is on earth. She is not a literal woman; she is a symbol. The career of the woman corresponds to that of Israel, for it is Israel that gave birth to Christ, who is the child (*Isa.*

9:6). This verse does concern the birth of Christ, but it does not concern us at all: rather, it concerns the nation Israel.

"Travailing in birth" is a figure associated with Israel: Before she travailed, she brought forth: before her pain came, she was delivered of a man child.

"She was delivered of a man child," meaning Christ. Therefore, we identify the woman as the nation of Israel.

"Being tormented," certainly Israel has suffered Satanic anti Semitism from the time of the birth of Christ to the present, in fact, even since before that day, because Satan knows that Christ would come from this nation.

The Red Dragon- Satan

And there appeared another wonder in heaven; and behold a great red dragon having seven heads and ten horns, and seven crowns upon his heads. And his tail drew the third part of the stars of heaven, and did cast them to the earth: and the dragon stood before the woman which was ready to be delivered, for to devour her child as it was born [Rev. 12:3-4].

"And there was seen another sign in heaven." Notice that these are signs that are given to us. They are not literal. If John is giving us a symbol, he will make it clear that it is a symbol. The red dragon is clearly identified as Satan in verse 9. *"And the great dragon was cast out which deceiveth the whole world; He was cast out into the earth, and his angels were cast out with him."* We can identify this character without speculating at all.

In this second sign, the true character of Satan is revealed with all the wrapping removed:

1. He is called *"great"* because of his vast power.

2. He is called *"red"* because of the fact that he was a murdered from the beginning (*John 8:44*).
3. He is called a *"dragon"* because of the viciousness of his character.

"Seven heads" suggest the perfection of wisdom that characterized the creation of Satan, who was originally the *"covering cherub."* Ezekiel 28:12 speaks of how he was at this origin. *"...full of wisdom and perfect in beauty."* This reveals two of the fallacies concerning Satan, having horns, cloven feet, and a forked tail. That's the *"great god"* Pan that the Greeks and Romans worshiped. That's not Satan, although Satan is back of that worship.

"Ten horns" suggests the final division of the Roman Empire, which is dominated by Satan and his final effort to rule the world. The crowns are on the horns, not on the heads, since it is delegated power from Satan. The crowns represent kingly authority and rulership.

The third of the stars of heaven indicates the vast extent of the rebellion in heaven when one-third of the angelic host followed Satan to their own destruction (see *Dan. 8:10; Jude 6*).

The dragon hates the man child because it was predicted from the beginning that the child would be the undoing of Satan. *"And I will put an enmity between thee and the woman and between thy seed and her seed: it shalt bruise thy head, and thou shalt bruise his heel."* (*Gen. 3:15*).

The Child of The Woman Jesus Christ

And she brought forth a man child, who was to rule all nations with a rod of iron: and her child was caught up unto God, and to his throne. And the woman fled into the wilderness, where she hath a place prepared of God, that they should feed her there a thousand two hundred and threescore days [Rev. 12:5-6].

The *"man child"* is Christ. He is easily identified here.

"Who is to shepherd (rule) all the nations with a rod of iron" is a clear-cut reference to Christ.

"Thou shalt break them with a rod of iron: thou shalt dash them in pieces like a potter's vessel (Ps. 2:9)."

Christ will come to put down all enmity, all opposition, all rebellion on the earth.

"And her child was caught up unto God and His throne." In the Gospels, the emphasis is on the death of Christ.

In the Epistle, the emphasis is on the resurrection of Christ.

In the Book of Revelation, the emphasis is on the ascension of Christ. The Book of Revelation is the unveiling of the ascended of Chris, the glorified Christ, the Christ who is coming in glory. The book of Revelation rests upon the fact of the Ascension. He is the One who has been opening the seals which have brought to pass everything that has happened since then.

"And she was delivered of a son, a child." Now this settles the identity of the woman. Israel is clearly the one from who Christ came. While the church came from Jesus Christ.

"And the woman fled into the wilderness where she hath a place prepared of (from God."

During the intense part of the Great Tribulation Period, this remnant of Israel will be protected by God.

Michael, The Archangel Wars with the Dragon

And there was war in heaven: Michael and his angels fought against the dragon; and the dragon fought and his angels, And prevailed not; neither was their place found any more in heaven. And the great dragon was cast out, that old serpent, called the devil and Satan, which deceiveth the whole world: he was cast out into the earth, and his angels were cast out with him [Rev. 12:7-9]

We have here a startling revelation: *"And there arose war in heaven."* It is difficult to imagine that there is war in heaven, but Satan still has access to heaven and as long as he does, there will be problems.

We are told in the Book of Job that Satan came with the Sons of God to appear before God (see *Job 1-2*). Satan apparently had as much right there as they did. Satan has access to God, and he is able to carry on a communication with God. "Michael is the arch angel; We are told this in the Book of Jude: *(Jude 9)*.

At that time, we are told, there will be a time of trouble, the Great Tribulation. Michael will again step out and drive Satan out of heaven because he happens to be the prince who watches over the nation of Israel.

There will be a fierce struggle, a war, Satan is not going to retire easily, but Michael and his angel will prevail, and Satan and his angel will be thrown out of heaven. Now Satan is not an ugly creature by any means: he is an angel of light. Notice how he is identified here:

1. He is called *"the old serpent."* This takes us back to the Garden of Eden. Satan is that old serpent, the one who was at the beginning in the Garden of Eden.

2. He is called *"Devil"* a name which comes from the Greek diabolos meaning *"slanderer or accuser."* Thank God that we have an advocate with the Father. Jesus Christ, the righteous is up there to defend us.

3. He is also called *"Satan"* which means *"adversary."* He is the awful adversary of God and of every one of God's children.

4. Finally, he is called *"he that deceiveth the whole nation (inhabited) world."* During the Great Tribulation, Satan will be able to totally deceive men – today, he deceives only partially. Satan deceives men relative to God and the Word of God. Satan deceives man relative to the world, the flesh, and the devil. We think we are big enough to overcome the world, the flesh, and the devil. Satan deceives man relative to the gospel. He doesn't mind a man going to church or even join a dozen churches, but he doesn't want man to be saved.

And I heard a loud voice saying in heaven, Now is come salvation, and strength and the kingdom of our God and the power of his Christ: for the accuser of the brethren is cast down, which accused them before our God day and night. And they overcame him by the blood of the Lamb, and by the word of their testimony; and they loved not their lives unto death. Therefore rejoice, ye heavens, and ye that dwell in them. Woe to the inhabiters of the earth and of the sea! For the devil is come down unto you, having great wrath, because he knoweth that he hath but a short time [Rev. 12:10-12].

"And I heard" this reminds us that John is still the spectator and auditor of these events. When Satan has been cast out of heaven, it will cause great rejoicing among the redeemed who are in heaven. (See *Rev. 6:9-10)*, for they mention their brethren on the earth: for the accuser of our brethren is cast

down. This opened the way for the coming of four great blood–brought, heavenly freedoms.

1. *"the salvation."* its consummation is in the person of Christ.
2. *"the power."* The nations have abused power; but it will be wonderful when Christ takes the power and controls the earth.
3. *"And the kingdom of our God"* will be established on the earth. Not until then will there be peace and righteousness and freedom on this earth.
4. *"And the authority (Gr: exousia) of His Christ"* shows that Christ has not yet taken over the government authority of this world.

Now all of these judgments are in preparation for His return to this earth, giving men a warning and an opportunity to turn to Him – and multitudes will. There is always a note of grace in the judgement of God. The one accusing them before our God day and night reveals that this is part of the present strategy of Satan, which attempts to thwart Christ's purpose with His church today and with the tribulation saints tomorrow. Victory for the accused saints comes through three avenues:

1. *"The blood of the Lamb."* There is wonder-working power in the blood of the Lamb. If any of us overcome, it will be through the blood of the Lamb.
2. *"the word of their testimony"* reveals that they were true martyrs. Those who are Christ cannot deny Him. These are the true martyrs. The Greek word martus means "witness." These are the ones who witness for Him.
3. *"They loved not their life even unto death."* This is an exalted plane to come to where we make the Lord Jesus the first love in our life. Love is the very basis of service.

There are two radical reactions to the casting out of Satan from heaven. There is rejoicing in heaven. Then there is woe on the earth. This is the third woe, that extends through the pouring out of the seven bowls of wrath. The only consolation for the earth is that Satan's sojourn on earth is a brief forty two months.

The Dragon Persecutes The Woman

And when the dragon saw that he was cast unto the earth, he persecuted the woman which brought forth the man child. And to the woman were given two wings of a great eagle, that she might fly into the wilderness, into her place, where she is nourished for a time, and times, and half a time, from the face of the serpent [Rev. 12:13-14].

This is the last wave of antisemitism that will rollover the world, and it is the worst, because Satan is cast down to the earth and knows that this time is short. He hates Israel because Christ came from this nation according to the flesh. This is the time of Jacob's trouble.

"Two wings of a great eagle" are given to her so that she might fly into the wilderness.

"Two wings of a great eagle" is not unusual or peculiar to the people of Israel but is reminiscent of God's grace in His past deliverance of Israel from Egypt. They come out because God brought them out and eagles' wings became a symbol to them.

In the Great Tribulation, the Israelites cannot deliver themselves and no one is interested in delivering them, But God will get them out as eagles' wings by His grace.

"Into the wilderness, into her place," we believe it to be a literal wilderness possibly that same one in which Israel spent forty years under Moses. This time it will be forty two months.

For that is the meaning of *"a time, and times half a time."* The important thing is not the place but the fact that God will protect them by His grace!

"Where she is nourished" reminds us that in the past, God sustained them with manna from heaven and water from the rock. He will nourish them again in possibly the same way.

And the serpent cast out of his mouth water as a flood after the woman, that he might cause her to be carried away from the flood. And the earth helped the woman, and the earth opened her mouth, and swallowed up the flood which the dragon cast out of his mouth [Rev. 12:15-16].

In the view of the fact that the wilderness is literal, the water also could be literal. God had delivered Israel out of the water, both at the beginning of the wilderness march at the Red Sea and then again at the end of the wilderness march at the Jordan River!

The Remnant of Israel

And the dragon was wroth with the woman, and went to make war with the remnant of her seed, which keep the commandments of God, and have the testimony of Jesus Christ [Rev. 12:17].

"The rest of her seed" may refer to the remnant who is God's witness in this period- 144,000 who have been sealed.

All antisemitism is Satan inspired and will finally culminate in Satan's making a supreme effort to destroy the nation of Israel. Satan has led the attack against the people because of the man child – Jesus Christ.

Chapter 13

Theme: *Wild Beast out of the Seas and Earth*

Wild Beast Out Of The Sea Description A Political Power And A Person

And I stood upon the sand of the sea, and saw a beast rise up out of the sea having seven heads and ten horns, and upon his horns ten crowns, and upon his head the name of blasphemy [Rev. 13:1].

Now, the better manuscripts today show the subject of the sentence to be he. Who is he? Whom were we last talking about in the previous chapter? He is the same person, and that, of course, is Satan.

"And I saw a (wild) beast coming out of the sea." Who brings him out of the sea? Satan brings him out of the sea. In scriptures, the sea is a picture of the nations of the world, of mankind, like the restless sea.

"Having ten horns and seven heads, and on his horns ten diadems, and upon his heads names of blasphemy." The dragon (Satan) stands on the sands of the sea, and it is he who brings the wild beast out of the sea and dominates him. This is Satan's masterpiece. The first beast is a person who

heads up the Old Roman Empire. Rome simply fell apart and this is the only one who will ever be able to put it together again. God is apparently taking His hands off this earth for a while and turning it over to Satan.

God must let Satan demonstrate that when he is given full sway, he will not be able to produce. This wild beast is similar in description to the fourth beast, that nondescript beast, in the seventh chapter of Daniel. There it represents the prophetic history of the Roman Empire, down to *"the little horn"* and his destruction. That fourth beast looked like it became dormant for a little while and then out of one of its seven heads, there came up ten horns, out of which came a little horn. The little horn put together three of the horns and was able to take the other seven.

At the time of John's writing, much of Daniel's prophecy had been fulfilled. The first three Beasts-Babylon the lion: Media-Persia, the bear; and Graeco-Macedonia. The panther had all been fulfilled. Now is John's day. It was fulfilled. Therefore, John centers on the fourth breast and upon the little horn because the fourth beast, the Roman Empire, had appeared.

However, in the Book of Revelation, the emphasis is on the rule of the little horn of Daniel? And the little horn is set before us as a wild beast. For he is now ruling and controlling the restored Roman Empire in John's prophecy. The little horn of *Daniel 7* and the wild Beast of *Revelation 13* are identical. Now you can see that an understanding of *Daniel 7* would be basic to understanding this passage.

The wild beast is the man of sin and antichrist, the final world dictation! The last verse of this chapter confirms this view (v.18). We are dealing with the man who is the world dictator at the end. But God has not been ready yet, and He will not let that one appear until the time of the Great Tribulation. Now the common market is interesting, not because we are seeing prophecy fulfilled; but because we are seeing the stage set which reveals that prophecy can be fulfilled. The common market (stock market) is just an interesting instrument.

The ten horns with ten diadems speak of the Roman Empire's tenfold division during the Great Tribulation. The horns are the ten kings who rule over this tenfold division. This interpretation is confirmed by *Revelation 17:12.* The little horn comes to power by first putting down three of these rules and afterward. He dominates the other seven and thus becomes the world dictator.

The seven heads are not so easily identified. But are interpreted in *Revelation 17:9-10* as seven kings. All seven heads are guilty of blasphemy. Blasphemy manifests itself in two ways: according to Govett:

1. Making one self equal with God, that's usurping His place and
2. Slandering and taking God's name in vain. The Romans were guilty of the first. The Pharisees were guilty of the latter. The beast here is guilty of both forms.

And the beast which I saw was like unto a leopard, and his feet were as the feet of a bear, and his mouth as the mouth of a lion: and the dragon gave him his power, and his seat, and great authority [Rev. 13:2].

John notes that he is a composite beast. We can begin now to formulate some very definite facts concerning Antichrist. He combines the characteristics of the other beasts representing kingdoms which Daniel saw in the vision of *Daniel 7:6.*

Some helpful points:

1. *"and the wild beast which I saw was like unto a panther."* The outward appearance of the beast was like a panther. This was the Graeco-Macedonian Empire (Greece).
2. *"And his feet were as the feet of a bear."* Reminds us of the second Beast of *Daniel 7:5.* This was Media-Persia.
3. *"And his mouth as the mouth of a lion."* Reminds us of the first Beast of *Daniel 7:4.* This was Babylonian autocracy.

Nebuchadnezzar was the head of gold. He was an autocrat. Through the man of Sin will be one of the toes of the image that Daniel saw, composed partly of clay and partly of iron, he will rule with autocracy and dictatorial authority of Nebuchadnezzar.

The final world dictator comes to his Zenith under the domination of Satan. The source of his power is found in Satan, who raises him up, empowers and energizes him for the dastardly dictatorial job he will do. Is the Man of Sin, the incarnation of Satan.

Wild Beast, Death- Dealing Stroke

And I saw one of his heads as it were wounded to death; and his deadly wound was healed: and all the world wondered after the Beast [Rev. 13:3].

Because of these two Scripture, many have taken the position that the beast is actually raised from the dead by Satan. This cannot be because Satan does not have the power to raise the dead; that power has not been given to him at all. The Lord Jesus Christ is the Only One who can raise the dead. Satan cannot therefore, the restoration is a false, a fake resurrection.

Others believe that the beast here refers to the Roman Empire and that the imperial form of government, under which Rome fell, will be restored in a startling manner. For Rome never died: Rome fell apart. Rome is like Humpty-Dumpty. But the Antichrist can and will put humpty dumpty together again and it will be a marvelous thing. The Roman Empire has not truly died. It lives on in the nations of Europe today.

There can be no real resurrection of an evil man before the Great White Throne judgment. Only Christ can raise the dead- both saved and lost. Satan has no power to raise the dead. He is not a life-giver. He is a devil, a destroyer, a death-dealer. We believe the beast to be a man who will exhibit a counterfeit and imitation resurrection. This will be the great delusion, the big lie of the Great tribulation period. We are told that God will give them over to believe the big lie (see *2 Thess. 2:11*) and this is part of the big lie. They will not accept the resurrection of Christ, but they sure are going to fake the resurrection of Antichrist.

"And his stroke of death was healed." Shows the blasphemous imitation of the death and resurrection of Christ. The challenge in that day will be: What has Christ done that the Antichrist has not done? Nobody can duplicate the resurrection of Christ: they might imitate it, but they cannot duplicate it. Yet the antichrist is going to imitate it in a way that will fool the world. It is the big lie.

The Roman Empire will spring back into existence under the cruel hand of a man who faked a resurrection and a gullible world which rejected Christ will finally be taken in by this forgery. We now begin to get a composite picture of the antichrist. The rider on the white horse (see *Rev. 6)* brought a false peace to the world.

"One of the paradoxes of this age is that this is the age of Pacifism but not the age of Peace." The antichrist comes in on a false platform of bringing peace to the world. That's all antichrists will need to offer the world when

he comes. He will say, *"I am going to give you peace"* and the people will say *"Hallelujah"* and put him into office. The world will put antichrist into power.

Wild Beast, Deity Assumed

And they worshipped the dragon which gave power unto the beast: and they worshipped the beast, saying, who is like unto the beast? Who is able to make war with him? [Rev. 13:4].

This is the supreme moment for Satan. He wants to be worshipped and the whole world is going to worship him during this period. If the spirit of God took His hand off the world today and off you and I. Many of us would be in the position of backsliders: and if the Antichrist appeared, we would follow him like a little faithful dog fellows his master.

"And they worshipped the beast, saying who is like unto the beast" What a parody on the worship of the true God. They say, *"Look we are worshipping the same thing more wonderful than the God of the Bible."*

And there was given unto him a mouth speaking great things and blasphemies; and power was given unto him to continue forty and two months [Rev. 13:5].

The only good news here is that the antichrist will be reigning like this for only forty-two months, or three and one half years.

"A mouth speaking great things" means he is a big mouth fellow. Daniel also mentions this concerning him. We need to test everything that we hear. The Antichrist is going to have charisma. He is going to be able to talk himself into the good grace of this Christ rejecting world.

<u>Wild Beast, Defying God</u>

And he opened his mouth in blasphemy against God, to blaspheme his name, and his tabernacle, and them that dwell in heaven [Rev. 13:6].

This is the dreadful limit to which the beast goes in blasphemy. He is against Christ and His church which are in heaven. Thank God that the church is no longer on the earth.

And it was given unto him to make war with the saints, and to overcome them: and power was given him over all kindreds, and tongues, and nations. And all that dwell upon the earth shall worship him whose names are not written in the book of life of the Lamb slain from the foundation of the world [Rev. 13:7-8].

"And it was given unto him to make war with the saints." The saints (there will be saints during the Tribulation Period, although they are not, Of course, the church) will be overcome by the brutal beast. In the will of God, many believers, both Jews and Gentile, will suffer martyrdom.

"And all that dwell on the earth shall worship him. Every one whose name hath not been written from the foundation of the world in the Book of life of the lamb that hath been slain." This will be the darkest hour in the history of the world; and the church. Thank God, we will not be here. We will not be under the antichrist: I am looking for Christ to come.

-

Wild Beast, Defiance, Denied To Anyone

If any man have an ear let him hear. He that leadeth into captivity shall go into captivity: he that killeth with the sword must be killed with the sword. Here is the patience and faith of the saints [Rev. 13:9-10].

This is without doubt one of the most awe-inspiring statements in the word of God.

"If any man hath an ear, let him hear." Here again is the wedding of free will and election.

"If any man" – any man means any man. *"If any man have an ear"* – does not everybody have ears? Yes, but some people do not hear although they have ears. There are people who simply do not listen at all- they do not hear.

Now, *"Any man"* – that's free will; that *"haht an ear"* is election; and this is the way God used these two truths together.

"He that leadeth into captivity shall go into captivity: he that killeth with the sword must be killed with sword." What John is saying here is not for you and me because beginning with chapter 4, Revelation deals with future things beyond the church.

John is speaking to God's saints who will be in the world at that time. Remember that during the Tribulation, the Antichrist will be the world dictator. Men are not going to buy or sell without this permission. God will apparently withdraw from the world, and He will turn it over to Satan. Today, the Holy Spirit is in the world, and He curtails. He is holding back evil, although it may not look that way.

CHAPTER 13

The Wild Beast Out of the Earth – Description, A Religious Leader

And I beheld another beast coming up out of the earth; and he had two horns like a lamb, and he spake as a dragon [Rev. 13:11].

Now the first beast is a political leader. We come now to the second wild beast, the one who came out of the earth and is a religious leader. This wild beast is easier to identify than the first. After you establish who the first beast, it is not too much trouble to identify the second. The first beast comes out of the sea and the second comes out of the earth. What is the difference? The seas represent the peoples of the world. The earth from which this second beast arises is symbolic of Palestine, and it is naturally assumed that the second beast comes from Israel. He is a messiah and Israel would not accept him unless he had come from their land and was one of them.

"And he had two horns like a lamb." This suggests his imitation of Christ. The first beast is opposed to Christ. He is the antichrist. The second beast imitates Christ. He also is antichrist (considering anti meaning instead of): he poses as Christ. He has two horns like a lamb, but he is a wolf in sheep's clothing. He imitates the *"... Lamb of God which taketh away the sin of the world"* (John 1:29). Only the pseudo lamb does not subtracts sin: he adds and multiplies it in the world. He is a counterfeit Christ. He will do a lot of talking about loving everyone, but underneath he is a dangerous beast just as the first one was, deceiving the whole world.

The second beast is the epitome of all false prophets and he is an antichrist. It takes two men to fulfill the position that Christ fulfills. They do not fulfill it. But Satan needs two men to attempt even an imitation of Him.

Wild Beast, Delegated Authority

And he exerciseth all the power of the first beast before him, and causeth the earth and them which dwell therein to worship the first beast, whose deadly wound was healed [Rev. 13:12].

The second wild beast has a delegated authority from the first wild beast, which actually makes him subservient to him, but he is also on part with him. He has the same power. This second wild beast leads in a movement to exterminate the harlot of *Revelation 17,* which is the false church that will go into the Great Tribulation Period. The true church, which has now left the earth, is called the bride of Christ. Here we have the last vestige of an apostate church with all of its humanism.

The false prophet will offer the world something new to worship. The first wild best, the willful king, the man of sin, the last world dictator (see *Dan 11:36-39; Matthew 24:24; 2 Thess. 2:3-10).*

 "Whose wound of death was healed" reveals that both the first and the second beats are healer and miracle workers. This is the big lie, the *"strong delusion"* that is going to come to the world.

And he doeth great wonders, so that he maketh fire come down from heaven on the earth in the sight of men, and deceiveth them that dwell on the earth by the means of those miracles which he had power to do in the sight of the beast; saying to them that dwell on the earth, that they should make an image to the beast, which had the wound by a sword, and did live [Rev. 13:13-14].

This false prophet is a worker of signs and miracles (see *Matt. 24:24).* Our Lord warned against this false prophet. This beast in the end time will also have satanic power. The false prophet shows his hand by causing to be made an image of the man of sin. The Greek word for image is eikon which means *"likeness,"* The big production is a likeness of the first beast that emphasizes the wound of death that was healed.

Wild Beast, Delusion Perpetrated On The World

And he had power to give life unto the image of the beast, that the image of the beast should both speak, and cause that as many as would not worship the image of the beast should be killed. And he causeth all, both small and great, rich and poor, free and bond, to receive a mark in the right hand, or in their foreheads: and that no man might buy or sell, save he that had the mark. Or the name of the beast, or the number of his name [Rev. 13:15-17].

"And it was given to him to give breath (the Greek word is pneuma), to the image of the wild beast." This is going to be a different kind of idol. Isaiah and all the prophets mention the fact that idols cannot speak. But here is an idol that will speak. He is now wedding religion and business, for you will have to have the mark of the beast to do business. What is the mark of the beast? It is not given us to know. We are not told, but that has not kept many expositors from telling us what it is.

Wild Beast, Designation

Here is wisdom. Let him that hath understanding count the number of the beast: for it is the number of man; and his number is six hundred threescore and six [Rev. 13:18].

"Here is wisdom" seems to be a rather ironical declaration when we consider the maze of speculation that has been accumulated through the centuries on this verse.

The visible number of the beast and it meaning await the day of his manifestation. For you will not know who he is until you get to the Great Tribulation Period. We should not waste our time trying to identify a person by this number: Instead, we need to present Jesus Christ. Instead of spending time with antichrist. We need to spend time with Christ.

Chapter 14

Theme: *Looking to the end of the Great Tribulation*

Picture of The Lamb With 144,000

And I looked, and lo, a Lamb stood on the mount Sion, and with him an hundred forty and four thousand, having his Father's name written in the foreheads [Rev. 14:1].

"I saw" indicates that John is still the spectator of these events. The reel continues to roll, and the story continues to unfold. The *"lamb"* is the Lord Jesus Christ, as seen in chapters 5-7 and 12-13.

"Mount Sion" is in Jerusalem. This verse pictures a placid, pastoral scene that opens the millennial Kingdom upon this earth. The Lord Jesus is going to reign from Jerusalem. God called it the city of the great King and in *Psalm 2:6.*

"And hundred forty and four thousand." We believe to be the ones who were sealed back in chapter 7, although I recognize that there are some problems connected with this view. They came through the Great Tribulation like three Hebrew children came through the fiery furnace.

Notice that the Lamb is standing with them on Mount Sion. Although, He is in His person, the Lamb. He is also the shepherd. Remember that He started with 144,000 and that He came through the Great Tribulation with 144,000. He didn't lose one.

And I heard a voice from heaven. As the voice of many waters, and as the voice of a great thunder: and I heard the voice of harpers harping with their harps: And they sang as it were a new song before the throne, and before the four beasts, and the elders: and no man could learn that song but the hundred and forty and four thousand, which were redeemed from the earth [Rev. 14:2-3].

"I heard." John is not only a spectator but is also an auditor for this scene. The 144,000 join the heavenly chorus in the millennium. The 144,000 learns the new song and join the harmony of heaven. I heard the voice of harpers harping with their harps.

"The hundred and forty and four thousand which were redeemed from the earth" means that they have been purchased to enter the millennium on earth. They are not taken to heaven. Remember that this is a picture of the millennium on earth, and these will live on the earth. The unsaved are not going to live on the earth.

"And no man could learn that song, but the hundred and forty and four thousand were redeemed from the earth. No one can sing praises to God but the redeemed." My friend, no one but the redeemed are going to say God is good. We need to say that God is good. But heaven and earth are brought into marvelous harmony in this millennial scene. This is a contrast to chapter 13, where the earth is in rebellion against heaven under the beast. Here all is tranquility under the Lamb.

These are they which were not defiled with women; for they are virgins. These are they which follow the Lamb whithersoever he goeth. These were redeemed from among men, being the first fruits unto God and to the Lamb, And in their mouth was found no guile: for they are without fault before the throne of God [Rev. 14:4-5].

"We're not defiled with women: for they are virgins." What does that mean? They were unmarried. Well, during the Tribulation Period, the times will be so frightful that it will be wise not to get married. You remember that the prophet Jeremiah also lived in a critical period. God forbade him to marry *(Jer. 16:1-4).* The word of the Lord came also unto me, saying, Thou shalt not take thee a wife *(Jer. 16:1-4).*

Now considering adultery in the spiritual sense in the Old Testament, idolatry was classified as spiritual fornication. The classic example is in *Ezekiel 16.* Where we find God's severe indictment against Israel for fornication and adultery – which was idolatry. The 144,000 will also have kept themselves from worshiping the beast and his image during the Great Tribulation.

Therefore, the comment, *"These are they which were not defiled with women; for they are virgins "* probably refers to chastity in both the literal and spiritual sense.

"First fruits unto God and to the Lamb" has definite reference to the nation Israel *(Rom. 11:15-16).* So Israel is described as the first fruit, especially the 144, 000.

"In their mouth was found no lie" means that they did not participate in the big lie of the beast when he used lying wonders. They didn't fall for his lie.

"They are without blemish." Are they without blemish because the Great Tribulation has purified them? No. They are without blemish because they are clothed in the righteousness of Christ.

Proclamation of the Everlasting Gospel

And I saw another angel fly in the midst of heaven, having the everlasting gospel to preach unto them that dwell on the earth and to every nation and kindred and tongue and people, saying with a loud voice Fear God and give glory to him: for the hour of his judgement is come: and worship him that made heaven and earth and the seas, and the fountains of waters [Rev. 14:6-7].

"Another angel" denotes another radical change in the protocol of God's communication with the earth. This angel is the first in a parade of Six "Another" angels mentioned in verses 8-9,15, and 17-18. During our age, the gospel has been committed to men and they alone are the messengers of it (the gospel). At the beginning of the Great Tribulation, men are the messengers of God, as the 144,000 reveals.

Angels as well as men were the messengers of the Old Testament- *"...the word spoken by an angel was steadfast..."* (*Heb. 2:2*). The times are so intense in the Great Tribulation Period that only angels could get the messages of God through to the world. Angels are indestructible.

"Fly in mid heaven" was a ridiculous statement a few years ago. Now it's no longer a ridiculous statement to a generation that has been treated to television via satellite. And the angel who John mentions flying in mid heaven" will serve as a broadcasting station to the entire world.

"An eternal gospel," the question naturally arises, How is this the gospel since the word gospel means "good news?" Is this angel bringing good news? Yes, it is good news to those who are God's children, but it is bad news for the unbelievers.

"Fear God" is the message of this *"eternal gospel."* That is the message the writer of the Proverbs said that the fear of the Lord is the beginning of wisdom. This is God's final call before the return of Christ in judgment.

Pronouncement of Judgement on Babylon

And there followed another angel, saying, Babylon is fallen, is fallen, that great city, because she made all nations drink of the wine of the wrath of her fornication [Rev. 14:8].

"Fell, fell is Babylon." This second angel runs ahead and announces what is yet to come as though it had already occurred. The city of Babylon will evidently be rebuilt during the Great Tribulation Period. We believe that ancient Babylon will be rebuilt though not in the same location, and that judgement upon it, which is predicted in Isaiah, is to come.

The idolatry of Babylon is a divine intoxication that will fascinate the entire world. Babylon hath been a golden cup of the Lord's hand that made all the earth drunken. The nation has drunken of her wine. Therefore the nations are mad *(Jer. 51:7).* This is a judgment on Babylon that we are going to see: judgement upon religious Babylon in chapter 17 of Revelation and upon commercial Babylon in chapter 18.

Pronouncement of Judgement On Those Who Receive The Mark of The Beast

And the third angel followed them, saying with a loud voice, if any man worships the beast and his image, and receive his mark in his forehead, or in his hand, The same shall drink of the wine of the wrath of God, which is poured out without mixture into the cup of his indignation; and he shall be tormented with fire and brimstone in the presence of the holy angels, and in the presence of the Lamb. And the smoke of their torment ascendeth up for ever and ever and they have no rest day nor night who worship the beast and his image, and whosoever receiveth the mark of his name. Here is the patience of the saints: here are they that keep the commandments of God, and the faith of Jesus [Rev. 9-12].

He is speaking to a group of people who *"keep the commandments of God,"* The Old Testament law scripture tells us that sacrifices will be brought during the Great Tribulation and even into the millennium.

"He also shall drink of the wine of the wrath of God." If you believe that the church is going through the Great Tribulation, you also believe that the Lord Jesus Christ is going to subject His own to the mingled, unmixed cup or His anger. I can't believe Christ would do this to the church (Bride), which He has redeemed.

"The wine of the wrath of God," is a figure adopted from the Old Testament *(Psalm 75:8)*. The Old Testament prophets picked up that theme. They saw the cup of wrath filling up to the brim. God was patient and let man go on and on in his sin, but when the cup of wrath was filled, then God would press it to the lips of a godless society. Rebellious men kept building this thing up until judgment had to break.

"Tormented with fire and brimstone." This is literal but if not, it is a symbol. Remember a symbol is used to give a faint representation of the real but just remember the brimstone of Sodom was literal. All God's own can do during the period is be patient and wait for the coming of Christ.

Now, why will we endure? We will endure because the Spirit of God has sealed us, and we are clothed in the righteousness of Christ. We can overcome by the blood of the Lamb. All they can do is wait out the storm, which is what they will do during the Great Tribulation.

He is speaking to a group of people who *"keep the commandments of God"* the Old Testament law. Scripture tells us that sacrifices will be brought during the Great Tribulation and even into the millennium.

"He also shall drink of the wine of the wrath of God." If you believe that the church is going through the Great Tribulation, you also believe that the Lord Jesus Christ will subject His anger. I can't believe Christ would do this to the church (bride), which He has redeemed.

Praise For Those Who Died In The Lord

And I heard a voice from heaven saying unto me, Write, blessed are the dead which die in the Lord from henceforth: Yea, saith the Spirit, that they may rest from their labours; and their works do follow them [Rev. 14:13].

Apparently, many of God's tribulation saints, both of the 144,000 and the untold number of Gentiles that will be saved. Many will lay down their lives for Christ. They will be martyred.

"For their works follow with them" reveals that they will be rewarded for their faithfulness, patience, and works in the period. Our God does not save

anyone for this works. Our works (good or bad) are like tin cans tied to a dog's tail. We cannot get away from them. They will follow us to the bema seat of Christ.

<u>Preview of Armageddon</u>

And I looked, and behold a white cloud, and upon the cloud one sat like unto the Son of man, having on his head a golden crown, and in his hand a sharp sickle [Rev. 14:14].

"I looked and behold" emphasizes the fact that John is not only a hearer but a spectator.

A white cloud, and upon the cloud one sat like unto the Son of man is evidently the Lord Jesus Christ. The cloud is a mark of identification. We believe that the clouds are shekinah clouds, which is the sign in heaven. On his head, a golden crown, further confirms this One as the Lord Jesus Christ. He is seen as King – not as prophet or priest. His office as King is always connected with His return to the earth.

"A sharp sickle" establishes this and speaks of the judgment of the wicked. The word sickle occurs only twelve times in the scripture, of which seven are in the verse of this section. Sharp occurs seven times in Revelation and four times in this chapter.

And another angel came out of the temple, crying with a loud voice to him that sat on the cloud, thrust in thy sickle and reap: for the time is come for thee to reap; for the harvest of the earth is ripe. And he that sat on the cloud thrust in his sickle on the earth; and the earth was reaped [Rev. 14:15-16].

"Send forth thy sickle and reap" refers to the judgment of men on the earth. Actually believers are not urged to harvest today; they are urged to sow, to sow the word of God. *"...a sower went forth to sow" (Matt. 13:3)* is a picture of Christendom today. The Lord Jesus Christ is the son of man. He is the sower and the seed is the Word of God and the field is the world. But there is going to be a harvest someday, but that will come at the end of age. We are not in the harvesting business. Our business is to sow the seed. We just sow the seed. Christ is the One who will have the harvest and the harvest is the judgement at the end of the age. Now, did this take place at the Lord's first coming ?No. It will take place at Christ's second coming to earth.

"For the hour is come to reap" conforms to the words of Jesus, *Matt. 13:39.* *"...the harvest is the end of the world."* Now let's make sure that we give out the Word of God and the Spirit of God will take care of the result. The time of harvest is set before us in the Old Testament *(Joel 3:13-14).*

And another angel came out of the temple, which is in heaven, he also having a sharp sickle. And another angel came out from the altar, which had power over fire; and cried with a loud cry to him that had the sharp sickle, saying, Thrust in thy sharp sickle, and gather the cluster of the vine of the earth; for her grapes are fully ripe [Rev. 14:17-18].

"The sanctuary which is in heaven" identifies this with the Old Testament, not with the church. The *"sharp sickle"* indicates judgment. *"Her grapes are fully ripe"* conveys the thought of their being day-like raisins. When Christ came the first time. He shed His blood for them, but they have rejected it. Now He is trodden down the wicked and it is their blood that's shed. He will gather them as we see *Revelation 16:16 "into a place called in the Hebrew tongue Armageddon."*

It is not a single battle but a war – the war of Armageddon (Heb: Har-Megiddon). This will be the sad end of that civilization which at the Tower of Babel demonstrated an active rebellion against God. You see, the *"gentle Jesus"* who wouldn't swat a fly, whom we have heard so much about, is just not the Jesus of the Word of God.

The Lord Jesus Christ is the Savior of the world but He is also the Judge of all the world. As a ripe grape is mashed and the juice flies in every direction, so will little man fall into the vat of God's judgement. This is Armageddon – the mount of the slaughter.

And the angel thrust in his sickle into the earth, and gathered the vine of the earth, and cast it into the great winepress of the wrath of God. And the winepress was trodden without the city, and blood came out of the winepress, even unto the horse bridles by the space of a thousand and six hundred furlongs [Rev. 14:19-20].

"Without the city" means outside of Jerusalem. *"Unto the bridles of the horses"* means about four feet deep.

"A thousand and six hundred furlongs" is about 185 miles, which is the distance from Dan to Beersheba. All of Palestine is the scene of the final war, which ends in what is called Armageddon. It is a campaign beginning about the middle of the Great Tribulation and is concluded with the personal return of Christ to the earth. *Psalm 45:3-7* is an Old Testament psalm. The only remedy for sin is the redemption Christ offered when He shed His blood on the cross and paid the penalty for our sins. The way out is to accept Christ.

Chapter 15

Theme: *Preparation for the final judgment of the Great Tribulation*

Tribulation Saints in Heaven Worship God

And I saw another sign in heaven, great and marvelous, seven angels having the seven last plagues; for in them is filled up the wrath of God [Rev. 15:1].

This will bring us to the end of the Great Tribulation Period. *"And I saw"* assures us that John is still a spectator of these events. He is attending the dress rehearsal of the last act of man's little day upon the earth.

"Another sign" connects this chapter with *Revelation 12:1*. The first sign, in the opening of chapter 12, was Israel. These seven angels of wrath are connected with the judgments to follow until Christ comes (see *Ch. 19)*.

From chapter 12 to the return of Christ is a series of mutually related events.

"Was finished" in the Greek language is in the prophetic aorist tease, which considers an event in the future as already accomplished.

"The wrath of God" marks the final judgment of the Great Tribulation. God has been slow to anger, but here ends His longsuffering. Judgment in the final stage of the Day of Wrath proceeds from God, not from Satan or the wild beast. It comes directly from God.

And I saw as it were a sea of glass mingled with fire: and them that had gotten the victory over the beast, and over his image, and over his mark, and over the number of his name, stand on the sea of glass, having the harps of God [Rev. 15:2].

"A glassy sea mingled with fire" represents the frightful persecution by the beast during the great tribulation period.

"And them that came off victorious" – here is the tribulation saints who have come through the fires of persecution on the earth and yet have not lost their song. They have the harps of God, and in the next couple of verses, we will see that they can sing and sing.

And they sing the song of Moses the servant of God, and the song of the Lamb, saying, Great and marvellous are thy works, Lord God Almighty; just and true are thy ways, thou King of saints. Who shall not fear thee, O Lord, and glorify thy name? for thou only art holy: for all nations shall come and worship before thee; for thy judgements are made manifest [Rev. 15:3-4].

If you want to learn *"the song of Moses"* you will find it in *Exodus 15:1-21* and *Deuteronomy 32:1-43*. Both songs speak of God's deliverance, salvation, and faithfulness! The song of the Lamb is the ascription of praise to Christ as the Redeemer. We have seen that in *Revelation 5:9-12*.

Again calling your attention to the fact that the Book of Revelation is Christ-centric that is Christ-centered. He is in charge; He is the Lord. In this book, we have the unveiling of Jesus Christ in His holiness, power, and glory.

"King of the ages" has two other rendering King of Saints and King of nations. There will be no place where He will not be worshiped.

"Who shall not fear, Lord, and glorify thy name?" In our day, there is very little reverential fear of God, even among believers.

"Nations shall come and worship before thee." The day will come when nations come and worship before the Lord. Jesus Christ. This is not true of nations today.

"For thy righteous acts were made manifest." This testimony coming from witnesses of this period is inexpressibly impressive and should settle in the minds of believers that God is right in all He does.

Tabernacle Opened In Heaven For Angels With Seven Bowls

And after that I looked, and, behold, the temple of the tabernacle of the testimony in heaven was opened: And the seven angels came out of the temple, having the seven plagues clothed in pure and white linen, and having their breast girded with golden girdles [Rev. 15:5-6].

The *"temple"* is referred to fifteen times in the Book of Revelation. It's prominence cannot be ignored. In the first part of Revelation through chapter 3, the church is the subject and there is no mention of a temple. Beginning with chapter 4, the scene shifts to heaven, and we see the temple in heaven; also there is a temple on earth patterned after the one in heaven; There is no temple in the New Jerusalem where the church is going. Why? Because the church is not identified with a temple.

And one of the four beasts gave unto the seven angels seven golden vials full of the wrath of God, who liveth for ever. And the temple was filled with smoke from the glory of God, and from his power; and no man was able to enter into the temple, till the seven plagues of the seven angels were fulfilled [Rev. 15:7-8].

The originals are referred to in *Revelation 11:19, "And the temple of God was opened in heaven, and there was seen in this temple the ark of his testament: and there were lightning and voices and thundering and an earthquake and great hail."* The action of God here is based on the violation of His covenant with Israel – the broken Law. God is righteous in what He is about to do. He will judge, then He will carry out His covenant with Israel.

Previously, seven angels blew on seven trumpets. Here is the new series of seven angels who have the seven plagues of the seven bowls of wrath. The angels' departure from the temple demonstrates that they depart from the throne of mercy and how God acts in justice instead of in mercy.

"Clothed in linen." The angels are clothed in linen- another meaning is clothed with precious stones. Through their garments identify them in a priestly activity, they forsake that work of mercy for plagues of judgment.

The *"golden girdles"* reveal the angels in the livery of Christ, who no longer is exercising a priestly function but is seen here judging the world.

"Seven angels seven golden vials." Again, let's call your attraction to the repetition of the number seven. It's said that seven is the number of perfection, which is not exactly accurate. For example, in six days God created heaven and earth and rested on the seventh day – not only because it was completed, but because it was perfect. But here in revelation the series of seven denotes a completion.

First in the seven seals, we see a broad outline. Then, as we read along in the prophecy, we see that God zeroes in and focuses on the last three and a half years.

"Bowls vials full of the wrath of God," notice they are not filled with the love of God but with God's wrath.

"The sanctuary (temple) was filled with smoke from the glory of God." This section refers to Israel, a people who had a tabernacle and a temple. The "seven golden bowls" represent the final part of the Great Tribulation Period.

These seven angels with priestly garments, having departed from the temple proper are no longer engaged in a service of mercy but are beginning a strange ministry of pouring out bowls of wrath on a Christ rejecting world. A world that has rejected the blood of Christ must bear the judgment for sin. This judgment is not the results of man's or Satan's enmity. It is the direct action of the Lord Jesus Christ. We have seen the gentle Jesus and now we see the wrath of the Lamb.

You never think of a little lamb as being angry. A lion can roar, but not a little lamb. The wrath of the Lamb is going to startle the world someday. The prophets of the Old Testament used the figure of the cup of iniquity and wrath filling up and spoke of God's patience in waiting for it to fill. Then, when it is full, God moves in judgement.

These seven angels with seven golden bowls make it clear that the judgment of the bowls proceeds from God and are not the result of man's mistakes or of Satan's enmity.

These judgements are the direct action of God.

Chapter 16

Theme: *Pouring Out The Seven Bowls*

Preparation For The Final Judgement of The Great Tribulation

And I heard a great voice out of the temple saying to the seven angels, Go your ways, and pour out the vials of the wrath of God upon the earth [Rev. 16:1].

Now there is a definite similarity between the judgment in this chapter and God's judgement upon Egypt through Moses. Remember that the Lord Jesus Christ is still in full charge. Remember that in chapter 5, the Lord Jesus was the only One found worthy to open the seven-sealed book, and His opening of the seals ushered in this entire series of sevens.

The Father has committed all judgement unto Him. Christ is the One who gives the command that sends out the seven angels with the final judgements. There is no longer a delay, no longer ad interval or intermission. The hour has come. The order is given and the seven angels execute the command.

"All of this beauty and glamour that we are seeing will pass away." It is under the judgment of God.

Pouring Out of The First Bowl

And the first went, and poured out his vial upon the earth; and there fell a noisome and grievous sore upon the men which had the mark of the beast, and upon them which worshipped his image [Rev. 16:2].

The angel leaves the place of the mercy seat in heaven and executes judgment. He leaves heaven and pours a judgment bowl of wrath on the earth. The first bowl of judgement is quite interesting. It looks as though God is engaged in germ warfare upon the followers of antichrist. Scripture states that the life of the flesh is in the blood, and death is in the blood. These purifying sores are worse than leprosy or cancer.

The first bowl of wrath compares to the sixth plague in Egypt, and is the same type of sore or boil (see *Exod. 9:8-12; Deut. 28:15).* Now the Book of Revelation, the "noisome and grievous sore" is for those who received the mark of the beast, those who did not receive the mark have been in a bad way. They have not been able to buy or sell.

But now, at the end of the Great Tribulation, those who have the mark and have enjoyed all the privileges it brought are going to be judged by God during the Great Tribulation. God's judgment of this terrible sore – which is probably worse than cancer – does not cause men to turn to God.

Pouring Out of the Second Bowl

And the second angel poured out his vial upon the sea; and it became as the blood of a dead man; and every living soul died in the sea [Rev. 16:3].

This plague is more severe than the second trumpet, where only one-third of the sea became blood. Here it is, the total seas and blood is that of a dead man! Blood is the token of life. *"For the life of the flesh is in the blood..."* *(Lev. 17:11).* The sea is a great reservoir of life. However, in the plague, blood is the token of death: the sea becomes a grave of death instead of a womb of life. Commerce is paralyzed. Human beings died like flies.

The first plague in Egypt was the turning of the waters of the Nile River into blood (see *Exod. 7:20-25).* There is a striking similarity here. The angels pour out the bowls in the days of God's wrath.

Pouring Out of The Third Bowl

And the third angel poured out his vial upon the rivers and fountains of waters; and they became blood. And I heard the angel of the waters say, Thou art righteous, O Lord, which art, and wast, and shalt be, because thou hast judged thus. For they have shed the blood of saints and prophets, and thou hast given them blood to drink: for they are worthy. And I heard another out of the altar say, Even so, Lord God Almighty, true and righteous are thy judgements [Rev. 4-7].

This plague, similar to the third trumpet, is again more severe. Only one-third of the flesh water was affected, and the total water supply of the earth will be cut off. This means the destruction of human life on an unparalleled plane.

"The angel of waters" is the superintendent of God's water department here on earth. This reveals another ministry of angels as it affects creation. This angel, who knows the whole story, now declares that God is right and holy in this act of judgment. Whatever God does is righteous and holy.

God is righteous in everything He does. They shed the blood of saints and prophets and blood didst thou give them to drink. Those who take the sword will perish by the sword. Those being judged had made martyrs of God's people, and now God is forcing them to drink blood for the righteous blood they spilled.

The altar saying evidently refers back to the saints under the altar who had been praying for justice to be done. Now here is their prayer to be answered.

Pouring Out of the Fourth Bowl

And the fourth angel poured out his vial upon the sun; and power was given unto him to scorch men with fire. And men were scorched with great heat, and blasphemed the name of God which hath power over these plagues; and they repented not to give him glory [Rev. 16:8-9].

Our Lord predicted signs in the sun during the Great Tribulation: *"And there shall be signs in the sun, and in the moon, and in the stars: and upon the earth distress of nations with perplexity: the sea and the waves roaring (Luke 21:25)."*

The Old Testament had a great deal to say about judgment during the Great Tribulation Period due to the excessive heat of the sun: *(Deut. 32:24)*. Also the prophet Isaiah speaks of this: *(Isa. 24:6 and Isa. 42:25)*. And back in the prophecy of Malachi we are told: *Mal. 4:1. "And men were scorched with great heat, and blasphemed the name of God."*

In spite of all of this, instead of turning to God for mercy, they blaspheme His name. This reveals that the human heart is incurably wicked. No amount of punishment will purify it and change it. The Great Tribulation is not for the purification of the church. Nowhere is it stated that the Great Tribulation is purifying the saints. Rather, it is a judgment upon the earth.

CHAPTER 16

<u>Pouring Out Of The Fifth Bowl</u>

And the fifth angel poured out his vial upon the seat of the beast; and his kingdom was full of darkness; and they gnawed their tongues for pain; and blasphemed the God of heaven because of their pains and their sores and repented not of their deeds [Rev. 16:10-11].

"The throne of the wild beast" makes it clear the first beast of chapter 13 is a man. He also represents a Kingdom, as you cannot have a King without a Kingdom.

"His Kingdom was darkened" indicates a strange darkness that might be called black light. The heat will be greater, but the light will be less. Note the similarity to the darkness of Egypt during the ninth plague *(Exod. 10:21-22).*

"They chewed their tongues from their pain." Just think of the intensity of the suffering that is caused by these bowls of judgment! But they don't turn men from their wickedness. There are two self-evident facts at this point:
1.   God is righteous in pouring out the bowls of wrath.
2.   Yet mankind is not led to repentance through suffering.

And here it is – the righteous judgment of God. And man continues to harden his heart and refuses to repent.

<u>Pouring Out of The Sixth Bowl</u>

And the sixth angel poured out his vial upon the great river Euphrates; and the water thereof was dried up, that the way of the kings of the east might be prepared [Rev. 16:12].

The Euphrates is called the great river in the Bible just as the Mediterranean Seas is called the great sea. The prominence of the Euphrates river in the world of God should not be overlooked. These verses before us are seen in connection with the sixth plague. It was the cradle of man's civilization and obviously will be the grave of man's civilization.

Abraham was called a Hebrew. Some interpret that as meaning he came from the other side of the Euphrates. The Euphrates River will be miraculously dried up, thus erasing the border between East and West, so that the Kings of the sun rising might come to the Battle of Armageddon.

Interlude: Kings of Inhabited Earth Proceed To Har-Magedon

And I saw three unclean spirits like frogs come out of the mouth of the dragon, and out of the mouth of the beast, and out of the mouth of the false prophet. For they are the spirits of the devils, working miracles, which go forth unto the kings of the earth and of the whole world, to gather them to battle of that great day of God Almighty [Rev. 16:13-14].

This is Armageddon (more correctly spelled Har-Magedon). It is not to be a single battle but a war, the war of Armageddon. It will be triggered. By the coming down of Russia from the north sometime around the middle of the Tribulation Period. It will continue for approximately three and one-half years. Here we are introduced to the trinity of hell – Satan, antichrist and the false prophet. They act in unison in forcing the nations of the world to march against Israel in an attempt to destroy God's purpose on earth.

"As it were frogs!" The question is will they be literal frogs? Well, they were literal in Egypt and they could be literal in this case but I am willing to accept them as a symbol. Notice that John says, *"as it were frogs,"* he doesn't

say they were frogs. They are spirits; they are *"unclean spirits."* They are *"demon spirits"* They are sent forth into activity by the Dragon Trinity!

The news media can brainwash the public. This is exactly what the trinity of evil will do. They will brainwash the nations of the world into marching against Israel.

Behold, I come as a thief. Blessed is he that watcheth, and keepeth his garments lest he walk naked and they see his shame [Rev 16:15].

"Behold, I come as a thief." Christ will never come as a thief to the church: *"But ye, brethren are not in darkness, that day should overtake you as a thief"* (1 Thess. 5:4).

A thief is someone you shut out; you don't welcome him. You never welcome a thief. You lock him out. Christ does not come as a thief to His church which is looking for Him. The Lord Jesus Christ does come as a thief to the world at the end of the Great Tribulation, as the verse before us indicates.

"Blessed is he that...Keepeth his garments." What garments are these? Be sure that you are clothed with the righteousness of Christ.

And he gathered them together into a place called in Hebrew tongue Armageddon [Rev. 16:16].

This is the only occurrence of the word Armageddon in Scripture, although there are many references to it. It means *"Mount of Megiddo."* It is a compound word made up of the Hebrew words Har, meaning *"Mountain,"* and Megiddo, which is a mount in the plain of Esdraelon.

"He gathered them together." The *"he"* is possibly God Himself. Although Satan (antichrist) and the False prophet act in unison to force the nation of the world to march against Israel, they nevertheless fulfill the Word of God.

Pouring Out of The Seventh Bowl

And the seventh angel poured out his vial into the air; and there came a great voice out of the temple of heaven. From the throne, saying it is done. And there were voices, and thunders and lightnings and there was a great earthquake, such as was not since men were upon the earth, so mighty an earthquake, and so great [Rev. 16:17-18].

"The seventh poured out his bowl upon the air." This is the last series of seven judgement before the coming of Christ, and this is the seventh and last of the last seven. In other words, we are right at the end of the Great Tribulation here. At this point, the only One who could deliver these people and set up a righteous Kingdom on earth and bring peace to the world is the Lord Jesus Christ. Let's keep our eyes on Christ. He is the judge now.

"Upon the air" means in space with no specific geographical location. The Lord Jesus Christ controls space. He is getting ready to come through space.

"The temple" has been mentioned again and again and again. It has been mentioned with the bowls of wrath, the trumpets and the seals, in fact, it has been mentioned with each series of judgements. The temple has been mentioned with the bowls of wrath six times – more than with all the other judgments combined – and this is the last reference to it. There is no temple in the New Jerusalem, so this obliviously has no reference to the church. Again, let's repeat that the church is not a part of this scene.

"A great voice came out of the temple, from the throne." That voice is not identified for us. But believe that it's the voice of the son of God. His message is recorded. It is done. This is the second time we have heard Him say this. When He was hanging from the cross, He said, *"It is finished."* In Greek, it is one word: Tetelestai. It is done. At that point in history, redemption was wrought, and salvation was finished for man. For those who have refused God's salvation, there is nothing they can do to escape the judgement of God. It is done. Now the writer to the Hebrews wrote *(Heb. 2:3).* How shall we escape if we neglect so great salvation: which at first began to be spoken by the Lord and was confirmed unto us by them that heard him.

Christ is the judge, and the judgement of the Great Tribulation is now concluded. *"It is done"* is His announcement, and there is nothing ahead but judgement, and Great White Throne judgment. Lightning, voices, and thunders were the solemn announcement at the beginning of the Great Tribulation that judgment was impending (See *Rev. 4:5).*

Now again, at the conclusion of the Tribulation are voices and thunders and lightnings. *"There was a great earthquake, such as was not since men were upon the earth."* The word of God makes it very clear that at the end of the Great Tribulation Period, there is to be a horrendous earthquake that will probably shake the entire world.

And the great city was divided into three parts, and the cities of the nations fell: and great Babylon came in remembrance before God, to give unto her the cup of wine of the fierceness of his wrath. And every island fled away and the mountains were not found. And there fell upon men a great hail out of heaven, every stone about the weight of a talent: and men blasphemed God because of the plague of the hail; for the plague thereof was exceeding great [Rev. 16:19-21].

This concludes the Great Tribulation Period. There is a great earthquake and it divides the *"great city"* of Jerusalem. The earthquake divides this city into three parts. Although the center of the earthquake is in Jerusalem.

"Babylon" is mentioned specifically again. It was mentioned in chapter 14, verse 8. The next two chapters give us the details concerning Babylon.

"Every island fled away" reveals that even the islands are shifted from one place to another by the earthquake. The final act of judgment is the hailstorm. The size of the hailstones is enormous – *"a talent weight."* The Greek talent was fifty-six pounds, and the Jewish talent was one hundred fourteen pounds. The miraculous hailstorm ends the Great Tribulation Period.

Chapter 17

🖋

Theme: *The apostate church in the Great Tribulation*

Great Harlot Riding The Wild Beast

And there came one of the seven angels which had the seven vials, and talked with me, saying unto me, come hither: I will shew unto thee the judgment of the great whore that sitteth upon many waters: with whom the kings of the earth have committed fornication, and the inhabitants of the earth have been made drunk with the wine of her fornication [Rev. 17:1-2].

"The great harlot" is that part of the church that will remain after the true church has been raptured. It will be composed of those who have never trusted Christ as Savior; they have never been in the Body of Christ. This is the group that enter the Great Tribulation. We are told certain things about her. She *"sitteth upon many waters."* According to verse 15, which we will see later, the *"waters"* refer to great masses of people and nations. The harlot will pretty much control the world!

"The Kings of the earth committed fornication" shows that there was an unholy alliance between church and state during that period. It will bring the world under the influence of the wild beast out of the seas and the wild

beast out of the earth! They will use the apostate church to control the masses, and the church will yield to this arrangement for political preferment and power.

"The judgement of the great harlot." God's cup of judgment will be pressed to the lips of the harlot. And who is going to destroy her? The beast himself will destroy her. Now the antichrist and the false prophet will not want her around after she has served their purpose. Antichrist wants to be worshiped and doesn't want any competition from the church.

So he carried me away in the spirit into the wilderness: and I saw a woman sit upon a scarlet coloured beast, full of names of blasphemy, having seven heads and ten horns [Rev. 17:3].

"He carried me away in the Spirit into a wilderness." We are told again John was in the spirit. Remember that this chapter is a vision where symbols are used. Around both Babylon and Rome, there is a literal wilderness.

John saw a woman *"sitting upon a scarlet colored wild beast."* This is a frightful and frightening scene. The wild beast has previously been identified as the antichrist ruling over the restored Rome Empire. The woman is identified for us in verse 18: *"And the woman who saweth is that great city, which reigneth over the Kings of the earth."*

The woman is a city, and the city is Rome, the world's religious capital. She is a religious Rome which at that time will have inherited all the religions of the world. All genuine believers, regardless of where they have gone to church, will be raptured. This will leave a church on earth that is totally apostate. Rather than being "the bride of Christ" God calls it a harlot.

The city is further identified in verse 9: *"And here is the mind which hath wisdom. The seven heads are seven mountains on which the woman sitteth."* Rome was a city set on seven hills, and was known as such to both pagan and Christian writers.

In these verses, the city of Rome is assuredly in view. The woman, the harlot, represents a religious system that will be revealed during the first part of the Great Tribulation Period after the true church has been removed from the earth.

"Full of names of blasphemy" reveals how far religion will have departed from the living Christ.

And the woman was arrayed in purple and scarlet colour, and decked with gold and precious stones and pearls, having a golden cup in her hand full of abominations and filthiness of her fornication: and upon her forehead was a name written, MYSTERY, BABYLON THE GREAT MOTHER OF HARLOTS AND ABOMINATIONS OF THE EARTH [Rev. 17:4-5].

"Clothed in purple and scarlet." Purple was the predominant color of Rome imperialism. Scarlet is the color accepted by Roman Catholicism.

"Gilded with gold" shows the beauty of the outward display, but, like the Pharisees, it is within *"full of dead men's bones and of all uncleanness."*

"Precious stones and pearls" are pretty cold, though they may be genuine, and are a sordid imitation of genuine heartfelt religion.

"A golden cup full of abominations" is the religious intoxication of the anti-church (not antichrist) and a pseudo-religion, counterfeit Christianity, a fake and false gospel, and a sham and spurious system. This is the cup

that makes the world drunk. Babylon hath been a golden cup in the Lord's hand, that made all the earth drunken: *the nations have drunken of her wine; therefore the nations are mad (Jer. 51:7).*

"Upon her forehead, a name written" is a startling revelation of the character of this woman. She does not wear a crown but rather the mark of her profession. The disgraceful title for the *"church"* which should belong to Christ as a bride. Babylon is the fountainhead for all false religion; therefore, she is *"The Mother of The Harlots And of the Abomination of The Earth."* This is a more expressive and vivid picture of awful abominable sin. Sex and false religions are related.

Have you noticed that this *"Mystery Babylon"* is called the *"Mother of Harlots?"* The mothers of harlots- not singular but plural. There will be more than the mother harlot – There will be a whole lot of harlots, a regular brothel.

And I saw the woman drunken with the blood of the saints, and with the blood of the martyrs of Jesus: and when I saw her, I wondered with great admiration. And the angel said unto me, wherefore didst thou marvel? I will tell thee the mystery of the woman, and of the beast that carrieth her, which hath the seven heads and ten horns [Rev. 17:6-7].

"Drunken with the blood of the saints." The harlot not only makes other drunk but she is intoxicated by her acts of persecutions.

"The saints" probably refer to Old Testament saints, and *"the martyrs of Jesus"* refer to New Testament saints. This indicates that *"Babylon"* is more than just Romanism. Rather, it is an amalgam of all religions. Babylon is a composite religious system. Babylon is the Old Testament persecuted God's

people and was the enemy of God. When John saw the vision of the woman, he says that he *"wondered with a great wonder."*

The angel asks why he should wonder when he (the angel) was present to explain the mystery of the woman. The emphasis here is on the Roman Empire aspect of the wild beast rather than on the antichrist aspect.

The beast thou sawest was, and is not; and shall ascend out the bottomless pit, and go into perdition: and they that dwell on the earth shall wonder; whose names were not written in the book of life from the foundation of the world, when they behold the beast, that was, and is not, and yet is. And here is the mind which hath wisdom. The seven heads are seven mountains, on which the woman sitteth. And there are seven kings; five are fallen, and one is, and the other is not yet come: and when he cometh, he must continue a short space [Rev. 17:8-10].

The wild beast *"was"* speaks of the past history of the Roman Empire. *"Is not"* refers to the present condition of the fragmented empire. The Roman Empire is not dead. It has fallen apart into the nations of Europe today.

"Is about to come up out of the abyss" speaks of the reactivation of the Roman Empire by Satan. Many have attempted to put the Roman Empire back together again but have never been successful. The wild beast, who is the antichrist, will be the one who put the Roman Empire back together again.

"Shall...go into perdition" speaks of the destruction of the Roman Empire by the coming of Christ.

"And there are seven Kings"

"The one is" refers to Domitian who was living in John day, who was also assassinated.

"The other is not yet come" refers to the antichrist. Other expositors (as Scofield Walter Scott) consider these seven as the different forms of government through which Rome passed!

Regardless of the interpretation adopted, the end in view is the same – the Antichrist rules over the reactivated Roman Empire.

And the ten horns which thou sawest are ten kings, which have received no kingdom as yet: but receive power as kings one hour with the beast. These have one mind, and shall give their power and strength unto the beast. These shall make war with the Lamb, and the Lamb shall overcome them: for he is Lord of lords, and Kings of kings: and they that are with him are called, and chosen, and faithful [Rev. 17:11-14].

At times the world beast signifies the last or eighth head: that is the individual emperor who is antichrist. Now here the antichrist is designated. He is the *"little horn"* in the vision that God gave to the prophet Daniel. The *"little horn"* puts down three other horns -that is , three kings -when he comes to power.

"The beast that was" refers to the past history of the Roman Empire. "And is not" refers to the end of Imperial Rome with its global empire, which came to an end and sometimes between the third and fifth centuries.

"Is himself also an eighth, and is of the seven" identifies the antichrist with the return to the imperial form of the restored Roman Empire. He is the *"little horn"* of Daniel, chapter 7. He is not one of the ten horns but he is

separate from them. He is an eighth head in the seven, yet he is one of the seven since he restores the last form of government to Rome.

The ten horns are the same as the ten horns of *Daniel 7:7*. These ten kings will reign with antichrist but will be subservient to him. They willingly give their authority to the antichrist and become his puppets.

And he saith unto me, the waters which thou sawest, where the whore sitteth, the peoples, and multitudes, and nations, and tongues. And the ten horns, which thou sawest upon the beast, these shall hate the whore, and shall make her desolate and naked, and shall eat her flesh, and burn her with fire. For God hath put in their hearts to fulfill his will, and to agree, and give their kingdom unto the beast, until the words of God shall be fulfilled. And the woman which thou sawest is that great city which reigneth over the kings of the earth [Rev. 17:15-18].

"The waters" are explained to be the many ethnological groups as well as the nations of the world. This figure is in harmony with that used in the Old Testament. The position of the harlot reveals that she is ruling over them for only a brief time.

"The ten horns" are ten kings as told us in verse 12, who rule over the different divisions of the Roman Empire. They, in turn, give over to the beast to lift himself up as a world dictator. For a time, the beast (antichrist) is willing to share his place of exaltation with the harlot since she has also sought to advance his cause while dividing the glory.

This he hates, and the ten kings are one with him in this. This great hatred destroys the fake church. It has no victory. Finally, it is destroyed by the antichrist. In doing this, the antichurch and his ten allies are fulfilling the word of God and carrying out His will, as did the Assyrian (as predicted in *Isaiah 10:5-19).*

By eliminating the apostate church, the way is cleared for the worship of antichrist as advocated by the False Prophet. The woman is a religious system, as we have seen. She is further identified as a city, the city of Rome. The reign and religion of antichrist is the darkest hour earth will know. Having rejected the truth, the only alternative left for man is to believe the big lie, the strong delusion. His story culminates in the catastrophic coming of Christ to this earth, as we shall see in chapter 19.

Chapter 18

Theme: *Political And Commercial Babylon Judged*

Announcement And Fall Of Commercial And Political Babylon

And after these things I saw another angel come down from heaven, having great power; and the earth was lightened with his glory [Rev 18:1].

Again we have the very interesting statement. *"After these things"* (Gr: meta tauta). After what things? After the series of sevens and after the judgment of religious Babylon come these things. Progress has definitely been made – through the seven seals, the seven trumpets, the seven personages, and the seven bowls of wrath – and we are advancing to the end of the Great Tribulation. In fact, this brings us to the end of the Great Tribulation.

John says, *"I saw."* He is still a spectator. He saw *"another angel,"* which takes us back to chapter 14, where a series of six angels is mentioned, each with the sole identification of *"another angel."* This angel is a divine supernatural messenger of God, but faceless and nameless. He has great authority (power), which indicates that he has a superior rank to the other *"another angel"* and he is bringing an important message.

"The earth was lightened with his glory," seems to further signify the prestige of this angel (cf. *Ezek. 43:2*)!

And he cried mightily with a strong voice, saying, Babylon the great is fallen, and is become the habitation of devils, and the hold of every foul spirit, and a cage of every unclean and hateful bird [Rev. 18:2].

The preliminary announcement of the fall of Babylon was made in *Revelation 14:8: "And there followed another angel, saying, Babylon is fallen, is fallen, that great city, because she made all nations drink of the wine of the wrath of her fornication."*

The angel here is greater in authority than the one who made the first announcement. In other words, *"Fell, fell is Babylon...and became."* The tense in the Greek is prophetic aorist which speaks of coming events as if they have already transpired. When God says something is going to happen as though it had already happened. Its' just that sure.

He knows the end from the beginning. Babylon this great commercial center of the world is going to be destroyed. A habitation of demons and a cage of every unclean spirit and hated bird. This indicates that Babylon is where demons of the spirit world and unclean birds of the physical world will be incarcerated during the millennium. The prophet Isaiah and Jeremiah confirm this (see *Isa. 13:19-22; Jer. 50:38-40*).

These prophecies find a final fulfillment in the destruction of literal Babylon here in Revelation 18. Babylon is the headquarters of demons and has been a place of rebellion down through the years.

For all nations have drunk of the wine of wrath of her fornication, and the kings of the earth have committed fornication with her, and the merchants of the earth are waxed rich through the abundance of her delicacies [Rev. 18:3].

"Have drunk" (or are fallen) are the two permitted renderings - both have good manuscript authority. Both true. The normal rendering is *"have drunk."* This is God's judgment on big business which denies God's authority. This is the unholy alliance of government and business.

The word for merchants means *"those who travel."* It is not those who produce good of manufacture goods, but those who are brokers, engaging in business for a big profit. This is true today of course. Man uses business as the biggest excuse for having no time for God, yet these same men must finally stand before God. God will judge godless commercialism.

And I heard another voice from heaven saying, Come out of her my people that ye be not partakers of her sins and that ye receive not of her plagues [Rev. 18:4].

This verse reveals that God's people are going to be in the world to the very end it is not speaking of the church which has already been removed before the Great Tribulation began. The One who is speaking in this verse is none other than the Son of God and He is calling His people out of Babylon before the judgment comes. Such was also God's warning to Israel in *Jeremiah 51:5-6, 45* and in *Isaiah 48:20.* The warning is twofold.

1.   They are to have no fellowship with the sins of Babylon and
2.   They are to flee before judgment falls.

If we will not deal with sins in our own lives here and now by confession and forsaking them. He will deal with it. Either He will judge sin now, or it will meet us at the judgement seat of Christ.

For her sins have reached unto heaven, and God hath remembered her iniquities [Rev. 18:5].

Babylon has a long history of accumulated sins, and God has the record. It is one of the oldest cities in the history of mankind and is probably mentioned more than any other city in the Bible, with the exception of Jerusalem.

Finally judgment breaks like a flood upon this city and its system. The judgment of God may be delayed but it is sure. It may seem to us that the unbeliever is getting by with sin, but God's judgement is coming.

Reward her even as she reward you, and double unto her double according to her works: in the cup which she hath filled fill to her double [Rev. 18:6].

This is poetic justice (see *Obad. 15).* The cups of iniquity is being filled to the brim: God is right and just in what He does.

How much she hath glorified herself, and lived deliciously, so much torment and sorrow give her: for she saith in her heart, I sit a queen, and am no widow and shall see no sorrow [Rev. 18:7].

You see, the prosperity of Babylon blinded her to the judgment of God: Luxury arrogance, pride, sin, and self-deception characterized the spirit of this godless city. World peace was in sight, and optimism was the spirit of the day.

Therefore shall her plagues come in one day, death, and mourning, and famine; and she shall be utterly burned with fire: for strong is the Lord God who judgeth her [Rev. 18:8].

This calls to us attention the suddenness of destruction and that it will be *"fire."* Death, mourning, and famine are the three horsemen who ride roughshod over Babylon. The destruction is total and final. In the scriptures, this is the city of prominence, but its long, eventful and sinful history ends with the judgement of God upon her.

"For strong is the Lord God who judgeth her." It is God who destroys this city because He alone is able to do it. Also, there will be the anticipation of joy in heaven because of the judgement of Babylon.

Anguish In The World Because of Babylon Judgement

And the kings of the earth, who have committed fornication and lived deliciously with her, shall bewail her, and lament for her, when they shall see the smoke of her burning. Standing afar off the fear of her torment, saying Alas, alas that great city Babylon, that mighty city! For in one hour is thy judgement come [Rev. 18:9-10].

In that day Babylon will dominate and rule the world. The capital of Antichrist will be Babylon and he will have the first total dictatorship. Everything that city will be in rebellion against almighty God and it centers Antichrist. In chapter 17, we saw that the Kings of the earth hated religious Babylon and that antichrist got rid of it in order that he might be worshipped without any competition in the area of religion. And the Kings of the earth joined in her destruction.

In contrast to this, here in chapter 18, we see that the Kings of the earth love commercial Babylon because of the revenue she brought to their coffers. They marvel at the sudden destruction of that which they thought was gilt-edged security. The judgment came in the space of one hour, reminding us of the sudden devastation caused by atomic explosion. This is a frightful picture presented to us. It's the final judgement that will bring Christ to the earth to set up His Kingdom.

And the merchants of the earth shall weep and mourn over her; for no man buyeth their merchandise any more; The merchandise of gold, and silver, and precious stones, and of pearls, and fine linen, and purple, and silk, and scarlet, and all thyine wood, and all manner vessels of ivory, and all manner vessels of most precious wood, and of brass, and iron, and marble. And cinnamon, and odours, and ointments, and frankincense, and wine, and oil, and fine flour, and wheat, and beasts, and sheep, and horses, and chariots, and slaves, and souls of men. And the fruits that thy soul lusted after are departed from thee, and all things which were dainty and goodly are departed from thee, and thou shalt find them no more at all. The merchants of these things, which were rich by her, shall stand afar off for the fear of her torment, weeping and wailing, and saying, Alas, alas that great city, that was clothed in fine linen, and purple, and scarlet, and decked with gold, and precious stones, and pearls! For in one hour so great riches is come nought [Rev. 18:11-17].

The merchandise covers every place of business. The articles are for a society accustomed to the better things of the material universe. Even men were brought and sold including their souls. Right now there is many a woman selling her soul. "And merchandise of horse, and chariots and slaves (bodies) and souls of men. The merchants of these things who grew rich by her.

Shall stand after off because of the fear of her torment, saying alas, alas (See *Ezek. 26-27*).

And every shipmaster, and all the company in ships, and sailors, and as many as trade by sea stood afar off, and cried when they saw the smoke of her burning, saying, what city is like unto this great city! And they cast dust on their heads, and cried weeping and wailing, saying alas, alas that great city,

wherein were made rich all that had ships in the sea by reason of her costliness!
For in one hour is she made desolate [Rev. 18:17-19].

The third delegation of mourners is composed of those who are engaged
in the transportation, the great public carriers. They had become rich by
transporting the merchandise of Babylon. All of this has an application for
us. How do we see the luxury of this world. The great cities of the world are
passing.

Anticipation of Joy In Heaven Because Babylon's Judgement

Rejoice over her, thou heaven, and ye holy apostles and prophets: for God hath
avenged you on her [Rev. 18:20].

The viewpoint of heaven is entirely different. It is no funeral procession
there. Rather, it is the celebration of an anticipated event. The saints prayed
for it: the prophets of the Old Testament and the apostles of the New
Testament predicted it. Now all is fulfilled and there is joy because God has
exonerated His name. Judgement has come upon these things. What is your
heart fixed on today?

And a mighty angel took up a stone like a great millstone, and cast it into the
sea, saying, Thus with violence shall that great city Babylon be thrown down
and shall be found no more at all [Rev. 18:21].

Even heaven calls our attention to violence the suddenness and the complete
annihilation of Babylon. Like a stone that makes a big splash and then dis-
appears beneath the waves will Babylon come to an end.

And the voice of harpers, and musicians, and of pipers, and trumpeters, shall
be heard no more at all in thee: and no craftsman, of whatsoever craft he be,

179

shall be found any more in thee: and the sound of a millstone shall be heard no more at all in thee; And the light of a candle shall shine no more at all in thee; and the voice of the bridegroom and of the bride shall be heard no more at all in thee: for thy merchants were great men of the earth; for by thy sorceries were all nations deceived [Rev. 18:22-23].

"And the voice of harpers and minstrels and flute players and trumpeters shall be heard no more at all thee." See rock music will go out of style.

"And no craftsman of whatsoever craft shall be found anymore at all in thee." Factories will close down.

"And the light of a lamp shall shine no more at all in thee." All the neon lights of Broadway will go out.

"And the voice of the bridegroom and the bride shall be heard no more at all in thee." It's all over – no more marry and giving in marriage here.

"For thy merchants were the princes of the earth; for with thy sorcery were all the nations deceived." Satanism will increases more and more as we draw near the end of the age. It will be Satan who is going to deceive and blind people, just as he blinds many in our day. This city deceived the world with the worship of antichrist. This is the strong delusion.

And in her was found the blood of prophets, and of saints, and of all that were slain upon the earth [Rev. 18:24].

God's people got rough treatment in this city and God judged it. This is Satan's city and he was a murdered from the beginning. Babylon was a city that murdered. It's final crime was the slaying of God's people. In Edward

Gibbon's book: The Decline and Fall of the Roman Empire: In it he gives five basic reasons why that great civilization withered and died.

1. The undermining of the dignity and sanctuary of the home which is the basis for human society.
2. Higher and higher taxes.
3. The mad cause for pleasure: sports
4. The Building of great armaments when the real enemy was within. The decay of individual responsibility.
5. The decay of religion: faith fading into mere form.

Thank God, the sad story of man's sin will come to an end. This chapter concludes the frightful period which was labeled by the Lord Jesus Christ the Great Tribulation. In the next chapter, chapter 19 we will see Him coming to the earth to bring to an end this dark, doleful, and disastrous period. The total period is seven years. It is the *"seventieth week"* of Daniel prophecy. In the Old Testament, Daniel divided it, and in the New Testament, John divided it into two separate and equal periods of three and one half years each. Everything is in position. The church could be captured at any moment and the Tribulation could begin. But it may not for we know not the day or the hour.

Chapter 19

Theme: *Marriage of The Lamb And Return Of Church In Judgement*

Four Hallelujahs

And after these things I heard a great voice of much people in heaven, saying Alleluia; salvation, and glory, and honour, and power, unto the Lord our God [Rev. 19:1].

"After these things" (Gr: meta tauta) is an expression we first bumped into when John gave the division of the Book of Revelation in chapter 1, verse 19 – literally, *"these things that shall be after these things."* After what thing? After the church things. Chapter 4 opened with meta tauta, and we have been meta tautaing ever since. This is a chronological progression. Now we will see what will take place after the Great Tribulation. It's recorded in this chapter: the coming of Christ to the earth. He is the only One who can end the Tribulation. And so, this is the last occurrence of the expression. Meta Tauta.

"A great voice of a great multitude." In the worship scenes of chapters 5-7, we saw the elders, the church, and the uncounted numbers of angels and

created intelligence of all worshipping God. Now a great number of tribulation saints has been added to the chorus.

This is the first time they have been able to utter the great note of praise of the Old Testament -Hallelujah! This word occurs four times in the first six verses. This is its only occurrence in the New Testament. It is reserved for the final victory. It is interesting to note that hallelujah occurs frequently in the Book of Psalms. It means *"praise the Lord."*

Hallelujah is a fitting note of praise at this juncture in the Book of Revelation. My friend, this is that great day that is coming. The earth will be released from the Bondage of sin.

For true and righteous are his judgements: for he hath judged the great whore, which did corrupt the earth with her fornication, and hath avenged the blood of his servants at her hand. And again they said, Alleluia. And her smoke rose up for ever and ever. And the four and twenty elders and the four beasts fell down and worshipped God that sat on the throne, saying Amen; Alleluia [Rev. 19:2-4].

It is interesting to note that at the conclusion of all these judgments, in heaven, who have more perfect knowledge than you and I, are alike to say that God's judgments are true and right. If you don't think what God is doing is right, it is because you, not God, are wrong.

In these verses, we find a picture of the church in heaven saying, *"Hallelujah."*

"He hath avenged the blood of his servants at her hand." You see, believers are forbidden to avenge themselves (see *Roman 12:19*). The twenty-four elders, for the first time, sing Hallelujah. This is the last time the elders appear as such for the figure changes now, and the church is to become the

Bride of Christ. The word church means *"Called out."* Here on the earth, we are the church, the called out ones, but after we leave the earth, we are the bride.

And a voice came out of the throne saying, Praise our God, all ye his servants, and ye that fear him, both small and great. And I heard as it were the voice of a great multitude, and as the voice of mighty thunderings, saying, Alleluia: for the Lord God omnipotent reigneth [Rev. 19:5-6].

"A voice came out of the throne saying Praise our God." Notice that the call to praise comes directly from the throne of God because the Lord Jesus Christ is preparing to take control of this world. This is truly the Hallelujah chorus and the most profound paean of praise in the entire Word of God. But before Christ returns to the earth, there is going to be a wedding and you and I, as believers, will be part of it.

Bride of the Lamb and Marriage Supper

Let us be glad and rejoice, and give honour to him: for the marriage of the Lamb is come, and his wife hath made herself ready. And to her was granted that she should be arrayed in fine linen, clean and white: for the fine linen is the righteousness of saints [Rev. 19:7-8].

This will be the most thrilling experience that believers will ever have. The church that is the body of believers all the way from Pentecost to the Rapture will be present now to Christ as a bridge for a marriage.

The marriage takes place in heaven and this is a heavenly scene throughout.

Eph. 5:25-27; This is the picture of the relationship between Christ and the church. The marriage of the Lamb is come. Marriage is a marvelous picture of the joining together of Christ and the church. Notice that the Old Testament saints are not included – only the believers during the church age are included. Even John the Baptist designated himself as only a friend of the Bridegroom. He said, *"He that hath the bride is the bridegroom.." (John 3:29)*. The bride occupies a unique relationship with Christ. You see, Christ loved the church and gave Himself for it.

What is so wonderful is that we will know Christ and really know Him for the first time.

"The fine linen is the righteous acts of the saints." The wedding gown of the church is the righteous acts of the saints. Then why does John say that the wedding garment is the righteous acts of the saints? Well, the wedding gown will be used only once, but we will be clothed in the righteousness of Christ throughout eternity.

We as believers will appear before the judgment seat of Christ not to be judged for our sins in reference to salvation but for rewards. Therefore the good works are the wedding garment of the church. The church will reveal His glory. That is the age to come he might show the exceeding riches of His grace in his kindness toward us through Christ Jesus *(Eph. 2:7)*.

And he saith unto me, Write, blessed are they which are called unto the marriage supper of the Lamb. And he saith unto me, These are the true saying of God. And I fell at his feet to worship him. And he said unto me, See thou do it not: I am thy fellow-servant, and of thy brethren that have the testimony of Jesus: worship God: for the testimony of Jesus is the spirit of prophecy [Rev. 9-10].

Now the marriage of the Lamb will take place in heaven, but the marriage supper will take place upon the earth. Both Israelites and Gentiles who enter the millennium are the invited guest. The marriage supper is evidently the millennium. The angel puts God's seal on this scene: *"These are the true words of God."*

After acting as a scribe for this scene, John feels compelled to worship the angelic messenger. However, he is restrained from doing so. The angel is but a creature. Only God is to be worshiped. What a rebuke to Satan, the antichrist and the false prophet who wanted to be worshiped. And many people in our day who want to be worshipped. After the marriage of the Lamb in heaven, the next great event is the return of Christ to the earth.

Return of Christ as King of Kings and Lord of Lords

And I saw heaven opened, and behold a white horse; and he that sat upon him was called faithful and true, and in righteousness he doth judge and make war. His eyes were as a flame of fire, and on his head were many crowns; and he had a name written that no man knew, but he himself [Rev. 19:11-12].

What a thrilling scene this is! This is the great climatic event toward which all things in this world are moving today. It is the coming of Christ to the earth. The program as we have outlined it. Reveals that Christ's return to the earth takes place at the end of the Great Tribulation Period, right before the establishment of His kingdom.

Now the ways He entered the world the first time. He was meek and lovely. He was the Savior who died for sinners. Now in the verse before us, we see Him coming in His great glory. His coming will be the final manifestation of the wrath of God upon a sinful world. The rebellion of Satan, demons, and men is contained, put down and judged. He puts down all unrighteousness before He establishes His Kingdom in righteousness. And here in chapter

19, heaven opens to let Christ exit. The white horse on which He rides is the animal of warfare.

When Jesus was on earth, He rode into Jerusalem upon a little donkey which, through an animal of Kings, denoted peace, not war. He is called *"Faithful"* because He has come to execute the long-time program of God.

"He is called True" for he is inherently true. He has come to judge and make war not to die on a cross again.

"Now his eyes a flame of fire." Back in chapter 1, verse 14, His eyes were as a flame, as He walked among the churches judging them. But now there is a difference – *"his eyes are a flame of fire"* because He has come to judge the earth and put down it's unrighteousness.

"Upon his head, many diadems" indicates that He will be the sole ruler of this earth and His rulership will be a dictatorship. I assure you that.

"And he had a name. written that no man knew." What is this name that no one knew but Himself? He is giving four names here which correspond to the Gospels:

1. King of Kings corresponds to the Gospel of Matthew. Matthew presents Christ as King!
2. Faithful and True corresponds to the Gospel of Mark. Mark presented as the servant of God.
3. Word of God. What the Gospel of John called Him. The Word. In the beginning was the Word *(John 1:1)*.
4. The Son of Man corresponds to Luke Gospel. Jesus, the Son of Man.

Now notice the further description of Christ at His coming.

And he was clothed with a vesture dipped in blood: and his name is called The Word of God. And the armies which were in heaven followed him upon white horses, clothed in fine linen, white and clean. And out of his mouth goeth a sharp sword, that with it he should smite the nations: and he shall rule them with a rod of iron: and he treadeth the winepress of the fierceness and wrath of Almighty of God. And he hath on his vesture and on his thigh a name written, King of Kings, and Lord of Lords [Rev. 19:13-16].

Notice that His garment is sprinkled with blood and that He is treading the winepress of the fierceness and wrath of God. This picture takes us back to *Isaiah 63:1-6,* which we have quoted previously.

Obviously, this refers not to Christ's first coming but to His second coming, as described here in chapter 19.

"And he shall rule them with a rod of iron" takes us back to *Psalm 2:* He didn't get them at His first coming. How will He get them now? *(Psalm 2:6-9).* Thou shalt break them with a rod of iron. Thou dash them in pieces like a potter's vessel. The fury of His wrath at His second coming sharply contrasts to His gentleness at His first coming. However, in both is revealed the *"wrath of the Lamb."* The armies...in heaven are evidently the legions of angels that do His bidding.

The War of Armageddon

And I saw an angel standing in the sun; and he cried with a loud voice, saying to all the fowls that fly in the midst of heaven, Come and gather yourselves together unto the supper of the great God; That ye may eat the flesh of kings, and the flesh of captains, and the flesh of mighty men, and the flesh of horses, and of them that sit on them, and the flesh of all men, both free and bond, both small and great [Rev. 19:17-18].

Now we come to the end of the war of Armageddon and this concludes the final battles. If there is one passage of scripture that in revolting to read, this is it. You will notice that God included it at the end of His Word to remind us how revolting and nauseating the deeds of the flesh to Him. Men who live in the flesh will have their flesh destroyed.

It is frightful to rebel against God because He will judge you someday. This scene reveals the heart of man and how dreadful that heart really is.

Hell Opened

And I saw the beast, and the kings of the earth, and their armies, gathered together to make war against him that sat on the horse, and against his army. And the beast was taken, and with him the false prophet that wrought miracles before him, with which he deceived them that had received the mark of the beast, and them that worshipped his image. These both were cast alive into a lake of fire burning with brimstone. And the remnant were slain with the sword of him that sat upon the horse, which sword proceeded out of his mouth: and all the fowls were filled with their flesh [Rev. 19:19-21].

Now for the very first time, hell is completely opened up. What a frightful picture this is. The beast and the false prophet defy God right up to the very last. They dare to make war with the Son of God. It is preposterous that there is such a rebellion of man against God. The outcome is inevitable. The two arch rebels and tyrants, the antichrist and the false prophets have the questionable distinction of being the first two who are cast into hell. Even the devil hasn't been put there yet.

"The sword which came forth out of his mouth." What is that sword? The sword that comes from the mouth of Jesus is His word. It was His word that

created this universe. It is the Word of God that will save you. And the Word of God will destroy the wicked at the end of this age. Amen.

Chapter 20

Theme: *The Millennium*

Satan Bound One Thousand Years

And I saw an angel come down from heaven, having the key of the bottomless pit and a great chain in his hand. And he laid hold on the dragon that old serpent which is the Devil and Satan and bound him a thousand years. And cast him into the bottomless pit and shut him up and set a seal upon him that he should deceive the nations no more till the thousand years should be fulfilled and after that he must be loosed a little season [Rev. 20:1-3].

You will notice that the thousand years are mentioned two times in verses 1-3. They are mentioned a total of six times in the twentieth chapter. It is true that the millennium is mentioned only in one chapter.

Six times the thousand years are mentioned and here it is in relationship to Satan. His incarceration and total absence from the earth change conditions from darkness to light. He is the god of this age. He is the prince of the power of the air and his power and influence in the world are enormous beyond the calculation of any computer. His withdrawal makes way for the millennium.

Therefore we see that Satan's relationship to the millennium is this. He must be removed from earth's scene before it can take place. You cannot have an ideal situation with him loose.

"An angel...laid hold on the dragon." Satan's great power is reduced, for an ordinary angel becomes his jailor and leads him away captive (see *Jude 9; Rev. 12:7-9).*

"The Abyss" is a better description of the prison than *"the bottomless pit."* In either case, it is not the lake of fire, which we shall see in verse 10.

"After that, he must be loosed for a little time" is one of the imponderable statements of scripture. Why is Satan loosed after God once had him put in the abyss in chains? Why did God let him loose? God has a great purpose in it. This is the great problem of evil. Why has God permitted it? Well, we believe that God is working out a tremendous program which is the mystery of God yet to be revealed to us. It's going to be revealed someday and all He is asking us to do is to walk with Him by faith. We need to trust God and know that whatever He is doing is right. God had Satan incarcerated for one thousand years because there could not be a millennium without that.

Saints of the Great Tribulation Reign With Christ One Thousand Years

And I saw thrones and they sat upon them and judgement was given unto them and I saw the souls of them that were beheaded for the witness of Jesus and for the word of God and which had not worshipped the beast neither his image neither had received his mark upon their foreheads or in their hands and they lived and reigned with Christ a thousand years. But the rest of the dead lived not again until the thousand years were finished. This is the first resurrection. Blessed and holy is he that hath part in and first resurrection: on such the second death hath no power, but they shall be priest of God and of Christ, and shall reign with him a thousand years [Rev. 20:4-6].

Many will die for Christ in the Great Tribulation period, but they will live again and reign with Christ for one thousand years. The tribulation saints will trade in three and one-half years for one thousand years. Now the thousand years means a thousand years. It is literal.

An attempt to reduce to spiritualize this passage is to disembowel all scripture of vital meaning, interpreting scripture a reductio ad absurdum. It's all literal. The throne is literal. The martyrs, Jesus, the word of God, the beast, the image, the mark in their foreheads, hands are all literal. And the thousand years are literal. The Greek word for "resurrection is onastasei which means to stand up; a bodily resurrection. It is rather difficult for a spirit to stand up and those who spiritualize this section are at a loss to explain just how a spirit stands up.

This is the same word used by Paul in 1 Corinthians 15 for the resurrection of Christ and believers. *"And I saw throne and they sat upon them"* is the one statement that is not entirely clear. Who are *"they?"* It is my judgement that they must be the total number of those who have a part in the first resurrection, which includes the saved of all ages. Now the first resurrection began with the resurrection of Christ. Then it is followed by the resurrection (at the rapture) of His church. Some more than nineteen hundred years later— but before the Great Tribulation (see *Rev. 4).*

At the end of the Great Tribulation saints (the souls of them that had been beheaded for the testimony of Jesus and the Word of God and whosoever worshipped not the wild beast) and the Old Testament saints (see *Dan.12:1-2).*

The tribulation saints and the Old Testament saints will evidently reign on this earth with Christ.

"They shall be priests of God" refers to the entire nation of Israel. This was God's original purpose for Israel (*Exod. 19:6*). In the theocratic kingdom here on this earth, the entire nation of Israel will be priests.

In Scriptures, there is more prophecy concerning the millennium than of any other period. The Kingdom was the throne of the Old Testament Prophets.

Satan Loose After One Thousand Years

And when the thousand years are expired, Satan shall be loosed out of his prison and shall go out to deceive the nations which are in the four quarters of the earth, Gog and Magog, to gather them together to battle: the number of whom is as the sand of the sea. And they went up on the breadth of the earth, and compassed the camp of the saints about and the beloved city: and fire came down from God out of heaven. And devoured them [Rev. 20:7-9].

Although the entire Book of Revelation deals with the last things, especially do these last few chapters. Here is the last rebellion of Satan and man against God. The millennium is a time of testing of man under ideal conditions, as this passage demonstrates. As soon as Satan is released, great company who has been under the personal reign of Christ under ideal circumstances goes over to Satan.

The human heart alone remains unchanged under these circumstances; many will turn their backs on God and go after Satan. This seems unbelievable but what about today? This rebellion following the millennium reveals how terrible the heart of man is. Jeremiah said, "The heart is deceitful above all things and desperately wicked. Who can know it? *(Jer. 17:9)*. The nations of the earth again will come under the spell of Satan and will plot a rebellion. Because the rebellion is labeled *"Gog and Magog"* many Bible students identify it with the Gog and Magog of *Ezekiel 38-39.*

Now the war in *Ezekiel 38-39* relates to Gog and Magog I and the reference here in Revelation 20:8 is to Gog and Magog II. Although the name are the same, this is a different war, the last rebellion of Satan. Just because the two events involve the same name does not mean they are the same.

In verse 9, there is the dropping of the last *"atomic bomb."* It simply means that natural forces which destroyed Gog and Magog I will destroy Gog and Magog II. This last resistance and rebellion against God is as foolish and futile as man's first rebellion in the Garden of Eden. Here it is not the beginning but the ending of man's disobedience to God. It is the finality of man's rebellion. Nothing remains now but the final judgment.

Satan Cast Into The Lake of Fire And Brimstone

And the devil that deceived them was cast into the lake of fire and brimstone where the beast and the false prophet are and shall be tormented day and night for ever and ever [Rev. 20:10].

This is a most solemn statement and it is rejected by this lovey-dovey age in which we live. However, it is a relief to God's child to know that the enemy- both his and God's —will, at last, be brought to permanent justice. For instance, how are sins that men have committed sins in the spirit be punished in the body?

To be in outer darkness and the abyss is to be separated from God and to look back upon a life that has been misspent in this world. Fire is a very weak symbol of the reality of what it means to be lost to be separated from God for eternity. You cannot reduce these descriptions to something less than the reality because a symbol is always a poor representative of the real thing. The reality exceeds the description. Hell is a place: it is also a state. It is a place of conscious torment. This is the language of the Word of God- you cannot escape it.

Setting of Great White Throne Where Lost Are Judged

And I saw a great white throne and him that sat on it from whose face the earth and the heaven fled away and there was found no place for them [Rev. 20:11].

The Great White Throne is what men mistakenly call the general judgement. It is generally only in the sense that all the lost of all ages are raised to be judged here. All who are saved have been raised in the first resurrection. The second resurrection in which the lost are raised to be given an equitable, fair, and just evaluation of their works in respect to their salvation.

This is the Great White Throne and the holiness of this throne is revealed in the reaction of heaven and earth to it: from whose face the earth and heaven fled away." The one seated on the throne is the Lord Jesus Christ (see *John 5:22, 26-29*). What is the work of God? *John 6:29:* It is to *"...believe on him whom he hath sent."* They who have done evil come forth unto the resurrection of damnation and condemnation -that is the Great White Throne judgement.

And I saw the dead, small and great, stand before God; and the books were opened and another book was opened which is the book of life: and the dead were judged out of those things which were written in the books, according to their works. And the sea gave up the dead which were in it; and death and hell delivered up the dead which were in them: and they were judged every man according to their works {Rev. 20:12-13}.

Yes, my friend, you will be able to get a fair trial there. Your life is unfolded on tape and Christ happens to have the tape. When He plays it back, you will be able to listen to it, and it is not going to sound good to you by any means. Do you think your life can stand the test? The dead are classified as the small and the great. They are all lost, for evidently none have their names written in the Book of Life. They had never turned to God for salvation *(John 5:40)*. These folk standing before His throne had not come. These are books that recorded the works of all individuals.

God has the tapes. God keeps the tapes and He will play them at the right time. If you are saved, you will not stand before this judgement. Your works are to be judged as a child of God at the judgement seat of Christ. The Bema Seat will be for the purpose of reward (see *2 Cor. 5:10)*. The Great White Throne judgement is the judgement of the lost.

"And the sea gave up the dead that were in it." God will have no problem with that. After all, they are only atoms. He just has to put them together again. He did it once; He can do it again. The graves on earth will give up their bodies and hades, where the spirits of the lost go, will disgorge for this judgement!

And death and hell were cast into the lake of fire. This is the second death. And whosoever was not found written in the book of life was cast into the lake of fire [Rev. 20:14-15].

"death and hades were cast into the lake of fire." Sheol or Hades (translated as hell in the New Testament) is the place where the unseen dead and is divided into two compartments! Paradise and the place of torment (see

Luke 16:19-31). Paradise was emptied when Christ took the Old Testament believers with Him at His ascension.

All who stand at this judgment are lost, and we are told that they are cast into the lake of fire which is the second death. The Lord also called it "outer darkness." We believe this is symbolic of something worse than literal fire of outer darkness. It is eternal separation from God, for death means separation.

"Death" the great final enemy of man is finally removed from the scene. *"Hades"* the prison of lost souls, is likewise cast into the lake of fire. The lost are no longer in hades but in the lake of fire. This is where Satan, the wild beast, the false Prophet and their minions were consigned. If man does not accept the life of God, he must accept the only other alternative: eternal association with Satan.

God never created man to be put in this place, but there is no other place for him. Hell was created for the Devil and his angels. The second death means eternal and absolute separation from God.

Chapter 21

Theme: *Entrance Into Eternity Unveiled*

New Heaven, New Earth, New Jerusalem

And I saw a new heaven and a new earth for the first heaven and the first earth were passed away; and there was no more sea [Rev. 21:1].

"And I saw" is the oft-repeated statement of John to remind us that he was a spectator to all of these senses. He was a witness to the final panoramic scene, which ushers in eternity. The scripture clearly teaches that their present order of creation is to pass away in order to make room for a new heaven and a new earth. The Lord Jesus Christ Himself said, *"Heaven and earth shall pass away..." (Matt. 24:35).* The old creations were made for the first Adam. Christ, the Last Adam, has a new creation for His new creatures.

"Heavenly" does not mean they are going to heaven, but that heaven is coming to this earth. This is what we mean when we pray the so called Lord's Prayer, *"Thy Kingdom come...in earth, as it is in heaven (Matt. 6:10)."*

The chief characteristic of the new earth, as we have suggested, is the absence of the sea. The sea in the past has been a barrier and also a border

199

of mankind which in some cases has been good and in others bad. Also, the sea was an instrument of judgment during the flood. However, by the disappearance of the sea the population on the earth can be doubled again and again because of the increase of the land surface.

And I John saw the holy city, new Jerusalem, coming down from God out of heaven, prepared as a bride as adorned for her husband [Rev. 21:2].

This is the part which should interest us. I believe that the New Jerusalem is where those of us who are God's children will live! I saw the holy city, new Jerusalem, coming down from heaven from God, made ready as a bride adorned for her husband. This New Jerusalem should not be identified with the Old Jerusalem, the earthly Jerusalem. The New Jerusalem is the habituation, the eternal home that is prepared for the church. We have seen in *Revelation 19:7-8* that ushering in the millennial period, actually before Christ returned to the earth, was the marriage of the Lamb and the bride was the church. This passage fulfills what Paul wrote to the Ephesians *(Eph. 5:25-26)*.

At the judgment seat of Christ *[The Bema Seat]*, there will be the straightening out and the judging of believers. Everything that is wrong will have to be corrected. All sins will be dealt with there. Rewards will be given out. And He is going to cleanse the church with the Word *(Eph. 5:27)*.

This is the picture we are getting here in chapter 21. The holy city, the new Jerusalem, is coming down from God out of heaven adorned as a bride for her husband. The marriage took place before the millennium and the millennium is now over.

The marriage relationship is the most beautiful and wonderful relationship. It's the oldest ceremony that God has instituted for man. It goes right back into the Garden of Eden to the very beginning and it is all important. In Ephesians 5:18, Paul is talking here to believers who are filled with the Spirit. All of these instructions are for Spirit filled believers.

That is the only commandments in scripture in which you are required to do something about the Holy Spirit. *"This is a great mystery."* Paul says, *"..but I speak concerning Christ and the church (Eph. 5:32)."* In heaven, we are going to be like Him (see *1 John 3:2).* We are going to have glorified flesh like He has. We are going to be one with Him.

New Era

And I heard a great voice out of heaven saying, Behold the tabernacle of God is with men and he will dwell with them and they shall be his people and God himself shall be with them and be their God. And God shall wipe away all tears from their eyes and there shall be no more death neither sorrow nor crying neither shall there be any more pain for the former things are passed away [Rev. 21:3-4].

"Behold the tabernacle [tent] of God is with men." What is the tent? We are told by *John 1:14, "And the Word was made flesh and dwelt [pitched His tent] among us..."* That flesh was crucified on the cross and He was raised in a glorified body. We, too, are going to have glorified bodies and we are going to live with Him in the New Jerusalem.

"They shall be His peoples, and God Himself shall be with them and be their God." God shall wipe away every tear from their eyes. In the New Jerusalem, there will not be any more tears.

"And death shall be no more." That is going to be a very marvelous improvement. For the former things are passed away.

And he that sat upon the throne said Behold I make things new. And he said unto me, Write: for these words are true and faithful [Rev. 21:5].

He is going to make all things new! We see here the glorious prospect of all things made new.

And he said unto me, It is done. I am alpha and omega, the beginning and the end. I will give unto him that is athirst of the fountain of the water of life freely. He that overcometh shall inherit all things and I will be his God and he shall be my son [Rev. 21:6-7].

"I am the Alpha and the Omega, the beginning and the end." This identifies the speaker as the Lord Jesus Christ, as He was identified like this in the first chapter of this book. Believers in their new bodies thirst after God and the things of God and they will be satisfied. All believers are overcomers because of faith. *"He that overcometh shall inherit these things."* For whatsoever is born of God overcometh the world and this is the victory that overcometh the world even our faith *(1 John 5:4).*

"I will be God unto him and he shall be the son to Me." All the sons of God become Son through faith in Christ: But as many as received him to them gave the power to become the sons of God even to them that believe on his name *(John 1:12).*

They *"inherit all things"* because this was promised to the sons of God *(Rom. 8:16-17).* *"The son to Me"* is in the Greek moi ho huios. This is a very unusual expression. Vincent calls attention to the fact that this is the only place in John's writings where believers is said to be a son (huios) in relationship with God. Believers in the church are one of the peoples of God, but they are more. They are the sons of God in a unique and glorious fashion *(1 John 3:2).*

But the fearful, and unbelieving, and the abominable, and murderers, and whoremongers, and sorcerers, and idolaters, and all liars, shall have their part in the lake which burneth with fire and brimstone: which is the second death [Rev. 21:8].

There are several amazing features about this verse. First of all, the creation of the new heavens and a new earth did not reflect the status of the lake of fire and the lost. They are going into eternity just that way.

In the second place, there is no possibility of sin, which made man become fearful, unbelieving, liars, murderers, and all the rest ever breaking over the barriers into the new heavens and the new earth. Sin and its potential are forever shut out of the new creation.

Finally, the lake of fire is eternal, for it is the second death and there is not the third resurrection. It is eternal separation from God and there is nothing as fearful and frightful as that.

New Jerusalem Description of The Eternal Abode of The Bride

And there came unto me one of the seven angels which had the seven vials full of the seven last plagues and talked with me saying come hither I will shew thee the bride the Lamb's wife [Rev. 21:9].

What follows in verses 9-21 is a description of that city. We have seen the psychological or spiritual aspect of it as wonderful but this physical description is also worth contemplating. We must pause here to consider the relationship of the city to the citizens and the city proper to the church. The citizens are identified with the city in chapter 22, verses 3, 6, 19.

This passage describes the adornments which reveal something of the love and worth that the Bridegroom has conferred upon His bride.

And he carried me away in the spirit to a great and high mountain, and showed me that great city, the holy Jerusalem descending out of heaven form God [Rev. 21:10].

Certainly, this city has no counterpart among earth's cities which are built upon an earthly foundation and are built up from that base. This city comes down out of heaven. She originates in heaven and the Lord Jesus is the builder.

Having the glory of God: and her light was like unto a stone most precious even like a jasper stone clear as crystal [Rev. 21:11].

This city reveals the high purpose of God in the church, which is to bring *"many sons unto glory"* (see **Heb. 2:10**). The word translated *"light"* (phoster) is the Greek word for the source of light. The city is a light giver.

It doesn't reflect light as the moon nor does it generate light like the sun. The presence of God and Christ gives an explanation to this, as He declared, *"...I am the light of the world" (John 9:5)*. God is light.

The whole city is like a precious gem. This gem is likened unto a jasper stone. The *"Jasper"* is a transliteration of the word iaspis. Moffatt suggests iaspis could mean the modern opal, diamond or topaz. Most likely diamond. The diamond seems to fit the description. The New Jerusalem is a diamond in a gold mounting. This city is the engagement ring of the bride: in fact, it is the wedding ring. Its' the symbol or the betrothal and wedding of the church to Christ.

The Gates of The City

And had a wall great and high, and had twelve gates, and at the gates twelve angels, and name written thereon, which are the names of the twelve tribes of the children of Israel: On the east three gates; on the north three gates; on the south three gates; and on the west three [Rev. 21:12-13].

There are twelve gates to the city, three gates on each side. On each gate are the names of one of the tribes of Israel. This is very striking and immediately suggests the order in which the children of Israel camped about the tabernacle in the wilderness wanderings.

The Foundation of The City

And the wall of the city had twelve foundations and in them the names of the twelve apostles of the Lamb [Rev. 21:14].

This city has twelve foundations, and the names of the twelve apostles are upon them. The church today is *"...built upon the foundation of the apostles and prophets. Jesus Christ himself being the chief cornerstone"* (Eph. 2:20).

To these twelve apostles were committed all the writings of the church. These men preached the first sermons, organized the first church and were among the first martyrs. It's not honoring scripture to attempt to minimize the importance of the twelve apostles. To them, the church shall eternally be grateful. This is not to rob Christ of His place, for His is *"the chief cornerstone"* but the church is built upon the foundation which the apostle laid.

The Size And Shape Of The City

And he that talked with me had a golden reed to measure the city, and the gates thereof, and the wall thereof. And the city lieth foursquare and the length is as large as the breadth: and he measured the city with the reed, twelve thousand furlongs. The length and the breadth and the height of it are equal [Rev. 21:15-16].

First of all, let's examine the size of the city. Twelve thousand furlongs is given as the measurement of each side and the height of it. The text has twelve thousand stadia, meaning about fifteen hundred miles. Now consider the shape of the city.

"The city lieth foursquare" is the simple declaration of scripture. That would indicate that the city is a cube with fifteen hundred miles on a side. To enclose a cube measuring 1,500 miles on each side, the sphere's circumference would be about 8, 164 miles.

The thinking is that one will live inside this sphere, not on the outside. Here on the earth, we live on the outside. The Lord had to make the law of gravity to hold us on the earth, or we would be flying out into space. We walk on the outside here, but we will walk on the inside of the New Jerusalem.

The Wall of The City

And he measured the wall thereof, an hundred and forty and four cubits according to the measure of the measure of a man that is of the angel. And the building of the wall of it was of jasper: and the city was pure gold, like unto clear glass [Rev. 21:17-18].

The wall of the city is for protection. A walled city is a safe city. The New Jerusalem is safe and those who dwell therein dwell in safety. The walls signify that this city has achieved the full meaning of her name-peace. The walls are 144 cubits in height or about 216 feet. Beauty rather than protection is the motive in design. It is a wall with jasper built into it and is generally designated as a jasper wall. The hardest of substance and the most beautiful gem constitute the exterior of the city.

The Stone of Fire In The Foundation

And the foundations of the wall of the city were garnished with all manner of precious stones. The first foundation was jasper; the second, sapphire; the third, a chalcedony; the fourth, an emerald; The fifth, sardonyx; the sixth, sardius; the seventh, chrysolite; the eighth, beryl; the ninth, a topaz; the tenth, a chrysoprase; the eleventh, a jacinth, the twelfth, an amethyst [Rev. 21:19-20].

The twelve foundations of the city not only have the name of the twelve apostles, but they are twelve different precious stones. The most beautiful and costly articles known to man are precious stones. These stones express in human terms the magnificence of the city. Closely examining these twelve stones in the foundation reveals a polychromed paragon of beauty: a galaxy of rainbow colors.

1. **Jasper (Gr:iaspis)** its color is clear. Probably the diamond.
2. **Sapphire (Gr: sappheiros)** it's color is blue
3. **Chalcedony (Gr: chalkedon)** its color is greenish.
4. **Emerald (Gr: smaragdos)** its color is green.
5. **Sardius (Gr: Sardios)** it's color is fiery red.
6. **Sardonyx (Gr: sardonux)** its color is red.
7. **Chrysolite (Gr: chrusolithos)** its color is golden yellow.
8. **Beryl (Gr: berullos)** its color is green
9. **Topaz (Gr: Topazion)** it's color is greenish yellow.

10. Chrysoprasus (Gr:chrusoprasos) its color is gold green.

11. Jacinth (Gr:Huakinthi) it's color is violet.

12. Amethyst (Gr: amethustos) its color is purple.

The foundation of the New Jerusalem is constructed of the flashing brilliance of rich and costly gems.

<u>The City And Street of Gold</u>

And the twelve gates were twelve pearls: every several gate was of one pearl: and the street of the city was pure gold, as it were transparent glass [Rev. 21:21].

Notice that verse 18 also says, *"and the city was pure gold like unto clear glass."* We were told at the beginning of the description that this city is transparent. This is the thing that gave me the lead and the key to believe that we will live on the inside and that everything is transparent.

The fact that it is transparent gold means that the light can shine out. There will be nothing to hinder the light, not even the street.

<u>New Relationship- God Dwelling With Man</u>

And I saw no temple therein: for the Lord God Almighty and the Lamb are the temple of it. And the city had no need of the sun, neither of the moon, to shine in it: for the glory of God did lighten it, and the Lamb is the light thereof [Rev. 21:22-23].

God lights the new creation directly by His presence. After the entrance of sin into the Old creation, God withdrew His presence and darkness covered the face of the deep *(Gen. 1:2)*. However, in the new creation, sin is removed and He again becomes the source of light. Today the Lord Jesus Christ is the

Light of the world in a spiritual sense: *(John 8:12)*. In the new creation, He is the direct physical as well as the spiritual light. In the tabernacle, there was the golden lampstand which is one of the finest pictures of Christ. In the New Jerusalem is the golden lampstand.

The New Jerusalem possesses the genuine article- God in person. The New Jerusalem will be independent of the sun and moon for light and life. The one who is the source of light and life will dwell within the city!

New Center Of The New Creation

And the nations of them which are saved shall walk in the light of it: and the kings of the earth do bring their glory and honour into it [Rev. 21:24].

"And the nations shall walk amidst the light thereof." It does not say they will live there, but they will walk in the light of it. In other words, the New Jerusalem, instead of the sun and moon will give light unto the earth. *"And the kings of the earth bring therein glory into it."* It will not be their permanent abode, but they will come up there to worship. We are told that we are a priesthood of believers.

And the gates of it shall not be shut at all by day; for there shall be no night there [Rev. 21:25].

It is nonsense to say that the gates are not shut at night because there is no night. Therefore, he says that they will not be shut by day. In other words, they will throw away the key because there will be no danger.

And they shall bring the glory and honour of the nations into it. And there shall in no wise enter into it any thing that defileth neither whatsoever worketh abomination or maketh a lie but they which are written in the Lamb's Book of life [Rev. 21:26-27].

God has apparently accomplished His original purpose with man – fellowship. He now has a creature who is a free moral agent and who chooses to worship and serve Him eternally. There can be no night since the Lamb is the light and He is eternally present. The gates are not for protection and they are never close. Rather they are the badge or coat of arms of the bride. Notice that these gates are of pearl. The pearl of great price has been purchased at a great price (see *Matt. 13:45-46)*.

The merchants' man who brought that pearl was the Lord Jesus Christ, and the pearl is the bride. The Lord Jesus Christ paid a great price to buy the pearl. This pearl was formed from His side. Someone has said, "I got into the heart of Christ through a spear wound."

He was wounded for our transgression. He was bruised for our iniquities. The church will be the fairest jewel of all when He makes up His jewels (see *Mal. 13:17-18)*. The New Jerusalem will be the center of the new heavens and the new earth. The Lamb's Book of Life contains the Names of the redeemed of all ages. There is a great gulf fixed between the saved and the lost.

The greatest joy that will capture the heart of the redeemed will be that of abiding in the presence of Christ for eternity. This is heaven to be with Him. Revelation is all about Jesus Christ. He is the centerpiece of God's universe.

Theme: *River of the Water of Life, The Tree of Life; The Promise of Christ's Return: The Final Invitation.*

River of the Water of Life And The Tree of Life

And he shewed me a pure river of water of life, clear as crystal, proceeding out of the throne of God and of the Lamb. In the midst of the street of it, and on the either side of the river, was there the tree of life, which bare twelve manner of fruits, and yielded her fruit every month and the leaves of the tree were for the healing of the nations [Rev. 22:1-2].

Up to this chapter, the New Jerusalem seems to be all minerals and no vegetables. However, here are introduced the elements which add a rich softness to this city of elaborate beauty. There was a river in the first Eden that branched into four rivers. Although there was an abundance of water, it is not called the water of life. Eden was a garden of trees, among which was the Tree of Life. God kept the way open for many by the shedding of blood (see *Gen. 3:24*). In the New Jerusalem, there is a river of the water of life and the throne of God is its living fountain supplying an abundance of water.

"The tree of life" is a fruit tree bearing twelve kinds of fruits each month. There is a continuous supply in abundance and variety. There is a tendency to spiritualize the passage in Revelation and compare it to the fruit of the Spirit. There's no objection to that, provided we hold to the literal interpretation.

And there shall be no more curse, but the throne of God and of the Lamb shall be in it and his servants shall serve him. And they shall see his face and his name shall be in their foreheads. And there shall be no night there; and they need no candle, neither light of the sun; for the Lord God giveth them light and they shall reign for ever and ever [Rev. 22:3-5].

The first creation was blighted by the curse of sin, and this old earth on which we live today bears many scar marks of the curse of sin. The new creation will never be marred by sin. The throne of God and the Lamb are in the New Jerusalem.

"His servants shall do Him service" reveals that heaven is not a place of unoccupied idleness but a place of ceaseless activity.

"His name shall be in their forehands." Each person will bear the name of Christ. Our attention in this section is called to the direct lightning of the new creation. God is light. It is in eternity that the bride will reign with Christ.

Promise of the Return of God

And he said unto me, these sayings are faithful and true; and the Lord God of the holy prophets sent his angel to shew unto his servants the things which must shortly be done. Behold I come quickly blessed is he that keepeth the sayings of the prophecy of this book [Rev. 22:6-7].

The important thing to note is that when He says, *"And behold I come quickly."* He means rapidly. This is repeated again in verses 12 and 20. It is repeated three times here at the end. *"Behold I come quickly."*- not shortly or immediately or even soon.

These events that we have been looking at in Revelation beginning with chapter 4, take place in a period of not more than seven years, most of which are confined to the last three and a half years. The Lord Jesus puts His own seal upon this book: These words are faithful and true means that no man is to trifle with them by spiritualizing them on reducing them to meaningless symbols. Our Lord is talking about reality. At the beginning of the book, there was a blessing pronounced upon those who read and hear and keep these words.

In conclusion, the Lord Jesus repeats the blessing upon those who keep these words. This book is not to satisfy the natural man's curiosity but to live and act upon it.

And I John saw these things, and heard them. And when I had heard and seen, I fell down to worship before the feet of the angel which shewed me these things. Then saith he unto me See thou do it not: for I am thy fellow servant and of thy brethren the prophets and of them which keep the sayings of this book: worship God. And he saith unto me seal not the sayings of the prophecy of this book: for the time is at hand. He that is unjust let him be unjust still: and he which is filthy, let him be filthy still, and he that is righteous let him be righteous still, and he that is holy let him be holy still [Rev. 22:8-11].

Notice John's final and oft-repeated statement that he was both auditor and spectator to the scenes in this book. This is the method that was put down at the very opening of the book. John was so impressed that his natural reaction was to fall down and worship the angel. The simplicity and meekness of the angel are impressive. Though the angel identifies himself as a fellow servant of John and the other prophets. He was merely a messenger to communicate God's Word to man and he directs all worship to God. Christ is the centerpiece of the Book of Revelation – don't lose sight of Him.

"Seal not up the words of the prophecy of this book." Daniel was told to seal up the words of his prophecy because of the long interval before fulfilling it (See *Dan. 12:4*). In contrast, the prophecy given to John was even then in the process of being fulfilled! For nineteen hundred years, the church has been passing through the time periods of the seven churches given in chapters 2-3.

"He that is unrighteous. He that is filthy" – probably the most frightful condition of the lost is revealed here, even more so than at the Great White Throne judgement of chapter 20. The sinful condition of the lost is a permanent and eternal thing. The condition of the lost gets worse until each becomes a monster of sin. On the other hand, neither is the condition of the servant of God static. They will continue to grow in righteousness and holiness.

And behold I come quickly and my reward is with me to give every man according as his work shall be. I am alpha and omega the beginning and the end the first and the last. Blessed are they that do these commandments, that they may have right to the tree of life, and may enter in through the gates into the city. For without are dogs and sorcerers and whoremongers and idolaters and whosoever loveth and maketh a lie. I Jesus have sent mine angel to testify unto you these things in the churches. I am the root and the offspring of David and the bright and morning star [Rev. 22:12-16].

Now the church should know the program of God. Either the angel is bearing a very personal word from Jesus or else the Lord is breaking through and saying it's personally. Our Lord promises that He is coming again. That is His personal declaration.

He will personally reward each believer individually – those in the church at the rapture as well as those of Israel and the Gentiles at His return to set up His kingdom at the Millennium. Again the Lord Jesus asserts His deity. *"I am the alpha and the omega, the first and the last, the beginning and the end."* He said this at the beginning of Revelation and He concludes with it. Only blood washed believers have authority over the Tree of Life and access to the Holy City (see *Rev.1:7-12)*.

"Dogs" come off rather badly in scripture but because of dogs were scavengers in the ancient world. They were considered unclean and impure. Also *"dogs"* was the designation for Gentiles (see *Matt. 15:21-28)* and Paul label for Judaizers (see *Phil. 3:2)*. He is called "the root and the offspring of David" which connects Him with and morning star" to the church.

The Old Testament ended with the promises that *"the Sun of righteousness will arise with healing in his wings"* – that is the Old Testament hope (see *Matt. 4:2)*. But to us, He is the bright and morning star who will come at a very dark moment.

Final Invitation And Warning

And the spirit and the bride say come and let him that heareth say come and let him that is athirst come. And whosoever will let him take the water of life freely. For I testify unto every man that heareth the words of the prophecy of this book, if any man shall add unto these things, God shall add unto him the plagues that are written in this book: And if any man shall take away from the words of the book of this prophecy. God shall take away his out of the book of life, and out of the holy city, and from the things which are written in this book [Rev. 22:17-19].

The bride is the church. This is a twofold invitation – and invitation to Christ is to come and an invitation to sinners to come to Christ before He returns. The Holy Spirit is in the world today and He joins in the prayer of the church, which says, *"Lord Jesus come, come."* The Holy Spirit is performing His work in the world today in converting and convicting men.

He works through the Word and through the church, which proclaims His word. The invitation to me is to come and to take the water of Life *(Isa. 55:1)*. The Lord Jesus stood and said in *John 7:37, "If any man thirst let him come unto me and drink."* That is the invitation that goes out today."

Final Promise And Prayer

He which testifieth these things saith, Surely I come quickly. Amen. Even so come Lord Jesus. The grace of our Lord Jesus Christ be with you all. Amen. [Rev. 22:20-21].

"Yea: I come quickly" — not soon, but when these things begin to come to pass, He is even then at the door.

Come, Lord Jesus *"is the heart cry of every true believer."*

"The grace of our Lord Jesus Christ be with you all. Amen." The Old Testament ends with a curse, the New Testament ends with a benediction of grace upon the believers. Grace is offered to all, but if any man (regardless of his merit) refuses the offer which is extended, he must bear the judgement pronounced in this book.

Grace is still offered to man. It is God's method of saving sinners. Amazing grace. How sweet the sound. That saved a wretch like me ! I once was lost but now am found was blind but now I see.—John Newton.